C.P. Weaver & C.R. Weaver

STEAM on CANALS

DAVID & CHARLES
Newton Abbot   London   North Pomfret (Vt)

To my wife, Rodney's mother, for the encouragement
she has given us during the endless hours spent
searching for information both technical and practical.
                                                C.P.W.

British Library Cataloguing in Publication Data

Weaver, C. P.
    Steam on canals.
    1. Canal-boats – Great Britain
    2. Steamboats – Great Britain
    I. Title   II. Weaver, C. R.
    623.8′ 204   TC765

    ISBN 0-7153-8218-7

Typeset by Typesetters (Birmingham) Limited
Edgbaston Road, Smethwick, Warley,
West Midlands
and printed in Great Britain
by Biddles Limited, Martyr Road, Guildford
for David & Charles (Publishers) Limited
Brunel House   Newton Abbot   Devon

Published in the United States of America
by David & Charles Inc
North Pomfret   Vermont 05053   USA

(*Contents page*)
The Dalswinton boat of 1788, taken from a contemporary sketch by Alexander Nasmyth, who attended the historic trial on 14 October 1788. Though a fairly credible representation of the boat itself, the background is clearly imaginary, as are some of the passengers on the boat – one of whom is supposed to be Robert Burns. The 25ft × 7ft twin-hulled boat was propelled by tandem paddle wheels between the hulls. The boiler, which cannot have been very large, was in the further hull and is hidden by the paddle cases (*Science Museum*)

Contents

Introduction

None of man's creations has had a greater effect on his way of life than the steam engine, nor has any other attracted more widespread and lasting admiration. This may seem a paradox, man being by nature conservative and thus opposed to any rapid change, until the nature of the changes wrought by steam are examined a little more closely. The steam age did not, like so many other 'changes for the better', sweep away centuries of tradition and leave a vacuum. Rather it created its own traditions and ways of life which dovetailed into those it was beginning to displace. Nowhere is this better seen than in the history of steam propulsion on our rivers and canals, for although steamboats began to appear well before 1820 and were common by 1900, they rarely displaced the older, traditional craft and the men who worked them were immediately recognisable as members of the waterway community.

The British canal system proper made relatively little use of steam power for commercial craft. This was an inevitable consequence of the way in which the system had developed, for apart from the ostrich-like canal managements which were more concerned with scoring points off one another than in developing an efficient, integrated system that might compete with the new railways, the canals themselves were too small even when they were built. The 'wide' waterways (taking boats of about 14ft beam) were smaller than those that already existed in Europe, while the 'narrow' (7ft beam) canal was forever handicapped by the plain fact that a full crew was needed to work a boat carrying no more than 25 tons. Single steamboats were uneconomic and the frequency of locks made the operation of trains hauled by a steam tug impractical except in a few places. On the narrow canals, therefore, the steamboat was a rarity, a fact which adds greatly to its interest. From what has just been said, it will come as no surprise that the most numerous, and technically most successful, steam canal craft were operated by the more progressive managements of the larger waterways in the north of England.

It is all too easy to romanticise the age of steam, but to do so is not only to blind oneself to its very real faults but also to misunderstand the character of the men who created and sustained it. It was a hard age, one in which many were faced with the simple choice between work and starvation, but it was also an age in which there were fewer obstacles to individuality and initiative than there are today. The operation of canal and river craft was hard, dirty and often dangerous work, especially in winter. The advent of steam propulsion probably eased the lot of the average boatman because it freed him from the complications and dangers of horses, towlines and sails and made operation of the boat less dependent upon wind and weather. Having said that, it did not alter the basic pattern of working long hours – more than twelve hours a day in many cases – and at least six days a week in all weathers, not only working the boat itself but often loading and unloading it as well. One must not forget that on the average steamboat there would be at least an hour's preparatory work in the morning before setting out, and at least half an hour more after tying up for the night.

Although the family boat was common on inland canals by the time regular steam services began, there were few such steam craft. Most had an all-male crew, out of tradition on rivers but out of necessity on the canals, for the economics of canal boat operation demanded that a steamer be kept running twenty-four hours a day if possible. Despite the rigours of such a life, there was seldom a shortage of labour in the heyday of steam power. Boatmen were in many ways more fortunate than their con-temporaries shut up in 'dark, satanic mills'. Not only did they enjoy an outdoor life but the captain of a boat was virtually his own master, even if he worked for a highly organised company like Fellows, Morton & Clayton, and it was he and not the company who engaged and paid his crew. Each boat was more or less an independent concern and because they were paid by the trip there was the incentive to work hard and better their earnings. Moreover, it was a more secure occupation than that of the average factory worker who could be thrown out of work at a moment's notice.

The social history of our waterways is a complete subject in itself and one cannot do justice to it in a book which is primarily a technical survey of the steam age on our inland waterways. This we present in words and pictures, taking for our title that of a paper first presented more than fifteen years ago and enlarged several times since; the research behind that paper began almost thirty years ago. Though convenient and euphonious, it may seem too specific in the present context, for the 'canals' of our title include river navigations and lakes. For this we make no apology. Canals and rivers are almost inseparable, and it was on a Scottish loch that our first steamboat paddled its way into history nearly two centuries ago.

Even by restricting ourselves to the briefest account of each subject, there is much more left unsaid than is set down. Again, there are things that we would have liked to include but could not because we could find no illustration, or lacked essential details. To quote the most amazing instance, no photograph can be found of an Aire & Calder compartment-boat train with a pusher tug, despite the fact that such trains operated from 1864 until the early years of this century. Some of our illustrations will be familiar, but these have not, we feel, been used before in quite the same context. That a degree of duplication has to be regarded as inevitable, is a measure of the task facing the historian even when dealing with the recent past. It should be a reminder to us that the photograph taken today is an historical document tomorrow.

The era of the truly commercial steamboat drew to a close in the 1950s, rather too soon for the infant preservation movement to have much impact. Few original steamers were saved intact and only the steam launch – usually a more personal possession – is represented by any number of survivors. Many craft were converted to diesel power, whereupon their original machinery was scrapped; even when one of these vessels becomes available for preservation, it may now prove impossible to obtain authentic replacements. Nevertheless there are a number of praiseworthy restoration projects to record, notably those involving craft which have been recovered intact from the depths of certain freshwater lakes. These are all part of the continuing history of steam power and as such provide a happy ending to our story.

The Pioneers

Thomas Newcomen's atmospheric engine was a turning point in history. The first engine ever to develop mechanical work independently of wind, water or muscle power, it paved the way for the Industrial Revolution. The significance of this engine is obvious today but at the time it was hard to comprehend, and although the engine spread far beyond the British Isles within a few years of its perfection at Dudley in 1712, it did so only in the role for which it was developed. A quarter of a century was to pass before there were any serious proposals to use it for something other than pumping water, and among those proposals was one for a practical steamboat.

There are a number of unsubstantiated claims to have propelled a boat by steam before 1700, but the first published description of something that could actually have performed this feat is British Patent No 566 of 1737, granted to Jonathan Hulls. A native of Aston Magna, Gloucestershire, Hulls was a clock repairer in Chipping Campden. How he came to devise his steamboat we do not know, but it is recorded that a Mr Freeman

Jonathan Hulls (1699–1758), designer of the first practical steamboat (*Science Museum*)

of Batsford Park provided him with the sum of £160 to complete his work and obtain a patent. In it he described 'a machine for carrying Ships or Vessels out of, or into, any Harbour or River against Wind or Tyde, or in a Calm'. It was a steam tug powered by a Newcomen engine driving a set of paddles through a double-acting ratchet assembly. Hulls also foresaw the possibility of installing such machinery in an ordinary merchant ship. He is said to have started to build such a vessel, obtaining his machinery from the Eagle Foundry in Birmingham, but there is no evidence that it was completed. Perhaps he found that it was impossible to fit a large enough boiler at that early stage in the development of the steam engine. But whether or not he completed his boat, Hulls had described in its essential details a practical steamboat which was identical in principle with that which became the first to paddle its way across British water fifty years later.

This later boat was the product of three complementary talents. It was paid for by Patrick Miller, owner of Dalswinton House, near Dumfries. Miller had spent several years trying to interest the Admiralty in his scheme to equip warships with paddle wheels so that they could operate against the wind, and to demonstrate his ideas had built more than one manually powered experimental boat of which the most successful was twin-hulled with the paddles between the hulls, power being provided by a capstan. The engineer responsible for the engine of Miller's boat was William Symington, a native of nearby Wanlockhead who had already made a name by devising and patenting an improved atmospheric engine that enjoyed the benefits of a separate condenser without infringing the notorious master patent held by James Watt. In 1786 Symington had exhibited a model steam carriage, but although Miller had seen this, he did not consider that steam power could be applied to his paddle boat until prompted by James Taylor, tutor to his younger sons. Symington was thereupon engaged to build a small engine for installation in a boat provided by Miller, being assisted in this by Taylor.

The finished craft was tried out on Dalswinton Loch on 14 October 1788 and,

with several people on board, paddled its way fitfully across the lake with frequent stops to rally the boiler. When in motion it achieved a speed of less than 2mph. Had Miller been a patient man, this might have been recognised for the triumph it was, but unfortunately he had invited his friends and tenants to witness the trial, boasting that they would see him carried across his own lake at 5mph. When this did not happen, he accused Symington of making him appear a fool in front of his friends. Worse, from an historical aspect, was the fact that his tenants included Robert Burns; later writers tended to spend more time arguing about whether Burns was or was not on board and, if they mentioned the outcome of the trial, generally assumed that it had been a failure.

If the trial is examined scientifically, it is seen to have achieved all that could reasonably have been expected. The engine still exists, and calculation shows that it could have developed about 0.2bhp at the paddle wheels with an effective wheel speed of around 3mph. Calculations based on known dimensions of the boat suggest that this would have been enough to propel it at something under 2mph in still water. The weak point was the boiler, probably a small haystack or wagon type; this was too small to provide enough steam for continuous operation. Nevertheless, Symington had built a practical marine engine that was capable of propelling the craft in which it was fitted.

Miller agreed to the construction of a larger engine for installation in a boat on the Forth & Clyde Canal, work on which had started before the Dalswinton trial. It was completed in 1789, but its first trial was a disaster for Symington, again through Miller's impatience. Once again he invited all and sundry to witness the trial, but this time there was a mechanical failure and a furious Miller withdrew his support. Given a more patient patron, Symington might have produced the first commercially practical steamboat in the early 1790s.

The development of such a craft was made inevitable by another event of 1789, the storming of the Bastille on 14 July. Before long Britain and France were at war, and as might be expected the British Army requisitioned large numbers of horses and an equivalent quantity of fodder. As Britain's newly industrialised economy relied heavily on horse-drawn transport, these demands caused shortages and resultant inflation. A practical alternative to the horse was required, and it is no coincidence that by 1804 there had occurred the first wholly successful applications of steam propulsion to road, rail and water transport. The first to follow in Symington's footsteps was an 'uneducated mechanic' named Smith, who in June 1793 tested a vessel of his own design on the Sankey Canal at St Helens. This had an atmospheric engine driving side-mounted paddle wheels through a normal crank, in contrast to the ratchets used hitherto, and achieved 2mph in its initial trials. On a later occasion it went down the Mersey to Runcorn and then up the Bridgewater Canal to Manchester. Smith was ridiculed for his efforts – the fate of many an inventor who is slightly before his time. He replied that 'before twenty years were over they would see the Mersey covered in smoke', and in this he was only a year or so out.

Between 1794 and 1800, the Duke of Bridgewater experimented with one or more paddle tugs powered by an atmospheric engine made by Bateman & Sheratt of Manchester. It is not clear whether he was influenced by Smith's vessel, or whether the first of his tugs was in fact a rebuild of the latter, but it is clear that the duke recognised the potential savings from wholesale replacement of horses by steam propulsion. It was with considerable interest, therefore, that he followed Symington's third and last attempt to build a successful steamboat in 1801. This time he was financed by Lord Dundas, the Governor of the Forth & Clyde Canal, who wanted a boat capable of towing one or perhaps two loaded boats through the canal. Two boats were built, the first being abandoned when Symington realised that it was too small. The second boat was the famous *Charlotte Dundas*, which on 28 March 1803 towed two other craft through the canal, taking 9¼ hours to cover 18½ miles. It was the first time that a steamboat had shown itself capable of performing commercially useful work in a reliable and consistent manner. The Duke of Bridgewater had ordered a fleet of similar tugs, being convinced that Symington was on the

threshold of total success, but he died before this could be fulfilled and his executors promptly cancelled the order. Simultaneously, the Forth & Clyde proprietors decided that the wash from a steamboat would damage the banks and ordered the *Charlotte Dundas* to be laid up. It was a cruel blow to Symington, and he took no further part in the development of steam craft. His work had not gone unnoticed, however, for there is little doubt that both Robert Fulton and Henry Bell studied the design of *Charlotte Dundas* before designing their own highly successful craft a few years later. The year 1807 saw Fulton's *Clermont* establish the first regular steamboat service on the Hudson River, while in 1812 Bell's *Comet* began the first regular service in Europe on the River Clyde.

An ironic twist to the story of steamboats on the Forth & Clyde Canal brings us to the end of this section and to the first scientific investigation into the dynamics of a canal boat. The development of railways in the late 1820s alerted the Glasgow businessman Thomas Grahame to the sort of challenge that would face canal transport in a few years' time. He therefore began a study of steam propulsion applied to canal and river craft, both in Europe and the USA. He brought back from New Orleans the plans of an American river steamer and persuaded the Forth & Clyde to build two similar vessels for services both on the canal and across the Firth of Forth. The first of these was the *Cyclops*, launched in 1830. Simultaneously he heard of some trials that had been carried out to establish the power needed to propel a canal passenger boat at higher speeds than were then usual, and immediately carried out similar trials of his own with a special lightweight twin-hulled passenger boat constructed by a Glasgow boatbuilder named Hunter. The eminent engineer William Fairbairn was invited to take part, and in due course he published a detailed analysis. This showed that the wash produced by the boat increased substantially up to a speed of 6–8mph, but that it then diminished until at 12mph the boat was planing and required relatively little power to move it. Fairbairn suggested the construction of special steam-powered, twin-hulled craft capable of averaging 9mph and was

Patrick Miller (1731–1815) who financed Symington's first steamboats (*Science Museum*)

James Taylor (1758–1825), tutor to Miller's sons, who assisted Symington in the construction of the Dalswinton steamboat (*City of Glasgow District Libraries' Wotherspoon Coll*)

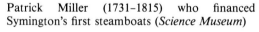

instructed to build two such vessels. The first, named *Lord Dundas*, was completed in January 1831. Notable for the extreme lightness of its construction, this appears to have done all that was claimed for it but made no lasting impression on canal passenger services. Fairbairn's idea of maintaining 9mph over a canal carrying ordinary commercial traffic was rather fanciful, and it was the twin-hulled horse-drawn 'Swift Boats' that saw out regular services on the Forth & Clyde. As Grahame had foreseen, canal packet boats were no match for the railway when it came.

While all this was going on, William Symington died, impoverished, in London, thus sharing a fate that befell Jonathan Hulls before him and would shortly befall his contemporary Richard Trevithick. In what other country are the men whose ideas laid the foundations for its national prosperity so shamefully treated? It is ironic, and tragic, to realise that the boat so admired by Thomas Grahame on his visit to New Orleans was virtually a direct copy of *Charlotte Dundas*, which lay rotting in a backwater of the Forth & Clyde Canal not thirty miles from his own home.

William Symington (1764–1831), son of a colliery engineer, the only man to bypass James Watt's separate condenser patent and designer of the first successful British steamboat (*Science Museum*)

9

(*above*)
Hulls's proposed tug of 1737. The vertical cylinder of the atmospheric engine is directly below the central pulley on the inboard shaft, and the piston is attached to a rope passing round and attached to this pulley. From the outer pulleys two further ropes are taken round the wheels on the paddle shaft and back over smaller pulleys (only one of which is shown) to a pair of hanging weights which are heavy enough to pull the piston back to the top of its stroke, as well as driving the paddle wheel through one of the ratchet drives mounted on the outboard pulleys. On the downward, power stroke of the piston, part of its energy is used to drive the paddle through the opposite ratchet, the ropes being taken round the pulleys in opposite directions, and part to raise the weights. The drive was thus continuous even though the engine was single-acting, and is typical of the ratchet drives used to produce rotary motion in the years before adoption of the crank (*Science Museum*)

(*opposite above*)
The engine of the Dalswinton boat was made by the Edinburgh brassfounder George Watt. It is the only surviving example of a Symington patent atmospheric engine, having been rescued by Bennet Woodcroft in 1853 and later reconstructed by John Penn & Son. As seen today, many major parts, such as the cylinders, are original but the exhibition standard of finish is not authentic. The twin single-acting cylinders operate the paddle wheels through double ratchet drives, exactly as in Hulls's design, being coupled together so that the engine is double-acting. There are two pistons in each cylinder, of which the upper is the normal power piston. At the bottom is the 'medium' piston, having a short stroke and separating the working volume of the cylinder from the integral condenser; by moving down as the power piston rises on the induction stroke, the medium piston expels air and condensate from the condenser. The two medium pistons are coupled by the small beam seen below the cylinders. The weight hanging at the side of the engine ensures that it always stops at the end of a stroke, ensuring an immediate start. The cylinders are 4in bore × 18in stroke, and at 18 strokes per minute the engine would have developed 0.2bhp (net) at a wheel speed equivalent to 3mph (*Crown Copyright, Science Museum*)

(*right*)
Charlotte Dundas was the first steam vessel able to produce a commercially useful performance in a reliable and consistent manner. This model is believed to be an accurate representation, with the possible exception of the boiler which looks a little too modern in concept. Adoption of the crank resulted in a much simpler engine layout than hitherto, but the double-acting cylinder still took steam at little more than atmospheric pressure and relied on condenser vacuum for its motive force (*City of Glasgow Museums and Art Galleries*)

10

"CHARLOTTE DUNDAS"
THE FIRST PRACTICAL STEAM VESSEL
DESIGNED AND ENGINED
BY
WILLIAM SYMINGTON.
1801-02
MODEL MADE FROM A PIECE OF WOOD OF THE VESSEL

(*above*)
The remains of *Charlotte Dundas* were photographed at Bainsford in 1856, shortly before the skeleton was broken up and, ironically, the very year in which the Forth & Clyde Canal finally adopted steam power for its commercial craft. Symington's historic boat had not moved under her own power since 1803, being laid up shortly after her triumphant haulage trials. For a few years after 1808, the hull was used for a manually operated dredger. There can be little doubt that this craft inspired both Henry Bell and Robert Fulton when they came to design their own steam vessels (*Glasgow Museum of Transport*)

(*opposite above*)
The first steamboat to be designed as a result of scientific investigation into the dynamics of a moving vessel, the twin-hulled passenger boat *Lord Dundas* entered service on the Forth & Clyde Canal in 1831. Designed by William Fairbairn in conjunction with the Glasgow boat-builder Hunter, who laid down the lines of the hull and probably erected the boat, it was 68ft long × 11ft 6in beam and weighed slightly over 7½ tons. The iron plates were less than ¹⁄₁₆in

thick. The 10nhp engine drove a 9ft paddle wheel between the hulls; at 50–60rpm it was expected to give the vessel a speed of 9–10mph. Ironwork and machinery were supplied by Fairbairn & Lillie of Manchester. *Lord Dundas* was expected by its designer to carry 150 passengers from Edinburgh to Glasgow at 2d per head (*Waterways Museum*)

(*right*)
The attractive little steam launch *Fire Fly* was one of the first private launches and is relevant to our story because she was fitted with a six-bladed screw propeller designed by John Ericsson shortly before his departure to the United States. It was powered by a two-cylinder oscillating engine with cylinders 3in bore × 6in stroke geared down to the propeller shaft. The machinery was made by Braithwaite, Milner & Co of London. *Fire Fly* was built for Henry Warriner of Bloxham Grove, near Banbury, and was kept on the nearby Sor Brook. Only 22ft long × 4ft 9in beam, she was delivered to Banbury under her own power and completed the journey on a local timber merchant's wagon. Her engine has survived and is now housed in the Science Museum (*J. C. Gibbard*)

12

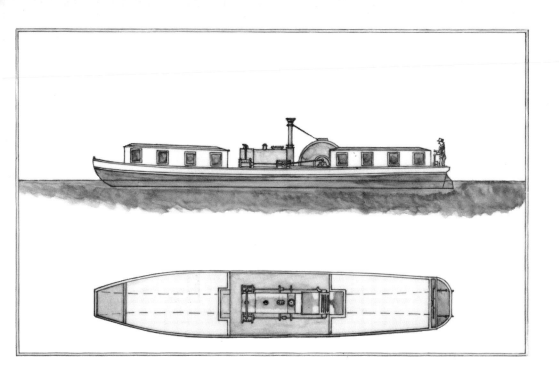

The Steam Narrow Boat

The cargo-carrying steam narrow boat was always something of a rarity because the space taken up by the smallest steam plant so reduced the carrying capacity that the boat became uneconomic unless it towed at least one other craft. Such operation was practical only on long, lock-free stretches of canal, or on a wide canal where both boats could use the same lock; thus the steam narrow boat was largely confined to the wide Grand Junction Canal and its narrow connections to Birmingham and Leicester. The most successful operator of such boats was Fellows, Morton & Clayton Ltd, who got results by working their craft really hard. Even so, the small FMC fleet fell somewhat short of the perfection with which legend has endowed it.

Attempts to perfect steam road vehicles in the 1820s led to the first light and compact steam engines capable of being fitted into a canal boat. Probably the first to install a steam engine into a narrow boat was John McCurdy, who in 1826 attempted a voyage from London to Oxford in a boat fitted with his patent 'duplex steam generators' and propelled by a rear-mounted paddle wheel that could be lifted inboard while passing through locks. The duplex generator was a form of flash boiler in which water was sprayed into a number of small iron cylinders set around the furnace, one of the first reasonably successful low-water-content, high-pressure boilers. In 1828 McCurdy made a successful trip from London to Manchester in the same boat, or one quite like it, and on this trip hauled a butty. His contemporary, David Gordon, the inventor of bottled gas, tried hard to establish regular steam services between London, Bristol, the Midlands and Merseyside in the late 1820s. Such plans were nullified by the overnight success of the Liverpool & Manchester Railway and subsequent railway construction.

In 1837 John Ericsson tested his newly invented screw propeller in a narrow boat fitted out by his good friends Braithwaite, Milner & Co. This boat, too, made a successful London–Manchester trip and subsequently operated a regular service over this route for a few months. Ericsson had failed by a few weeks to be the first with a truly workable screw propeller, and shortly after-

wards he emigrated to the United States.

Eight years later the Birmingham engineer James Inshaw built the first of his notable twin-screw canal steamers. Among his pupils who worked on later versions of this boat was William Stroudley, later to find fame as Locomotive Superintendent of the London, Brighton & South Coast Railway. Inshaw's success was due to the use of simple and well-tried equipment. Located right in the stern of the boat was a small locomotive-type boiler beneath which was the crankshaft of a two-cylinder horizontal engine, one cylinder lying either side of the boiler. From bevel gears at the outer ends of this shaft were driven the twin propeller shafts. The large blade area and low speed of Inshaw's twin propellers gave a high propulsive efficiency and the wash produced was correspondingly small in relation to the useful work done. This was demonstrated in 1859 when the Midland Railway, owners of the Ashby Canal, banned the Inshaw steamer *Pioneer* on the familiar grounds of bank erosion. The dispute went to the Court of Chancery, whereupon Mr W. Pole was engaged to investigate the MR's claims. He found that the wash was not damaging below 4mph, and the court ruled that steam craft should be permitted to operate subject to observance of a speed limit. This set the fashion for other waterways.

The success of *Pioneer* encouraged the Grand Junction Canal to build some steamers for its Carrying Department, set up a few years earlier and never really profitable. Their first boat, too, was named *Pioneer*, but it was a very different affair from its namesake. It was designed by Edwyn Elliott, who was the engineer in charge of the company's boat dock at City Road Basin. Elliott's machinery was more modern than Inshaw's and his layout established the classic form of motor narrow boat that has survived to the present day, the engine-room being a forward extension of the cabin. To save space, a vertical-flue boiler was used, which supplied steam at 75psig to a large single-cylinder engine. The vertical-flue boiler was a type that would not appeal to a present-day boiler inspector, for having an annular flue surrounding the circular firebox it was impossible to inspect much of the internal structure. The earliest

engines had cylinders 9in bore × 8in stroke (8nhp) and generally ran at about 180rpm, cut-off being 50 per cent. A large, two-bladed Griffith's propeller was fitted, this being an unusual design with a large spherical boss and blades angled forwards. Later boats had engines of 10nhp (8in × 10in) or 12nhp (7in × 12in). An idea of how they worked is given by the records for *Dart*, launched in 1864. In her first twelve months of service, she covered 11,280 miles, towing a butty, and carried 3,182 tons of cargo. This is equivalent to thirty-eight round trips between London and Birmingham with an average load of 42 tons, only one-third of which would be carried in the steamer. Though somewhat short of later Fellows, Morton achievements, this was still hard work and probably meant running round the clock with duplicate, all-male crews.

The GJCC's Carrying Department was never a success and came to an abrupt end in 1876 when the company counted the cost of the disastrous explosion in Regent's Park on 2 October 1874, caused by a spark from a GJCC steamer igniting a cargo of gunpowder. The effects of the Carrying Department were sold in October 1876 and included twenty steam 'tugs', as the cargo-carrying boats were officially termed. Most of them went to a new company headed by Joshua Fellows, this concern later becoming Fellows, Morton & Co. The fleet was gradually modernised, either by rebuilding the old boats or replacing them with new ones. A new design of engine was introduced, devised by their engineer, W. H. Haines. The 'Haines' engine was a vertical tandem compound, and may well have been produced by fitting a new high-pressure cylinder to the existing Elliott engines, the original cylinder becoming the low-pressure one. Compounding meant the use of higher steam pressures, and many of the early FMC boats had the newly patented Cochrane vertical boiler. In 1889 Fellows, Morton & Co amalgamated with two other concerns to form Fellows, Morton & Clayton Ltd. The steamer fleet was increased by four craft in this operation, these having two-cylinder simple engines though otherwise similar to the old GJCC craft, but of more importance was the acquisition of the Saltley

15

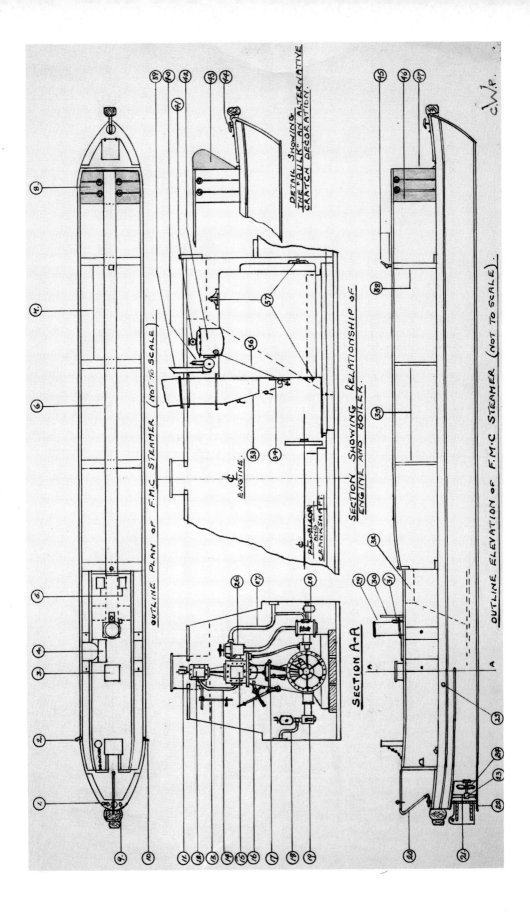

OUTLINE PLAN OF F.M.C. STEAMER (NOT TO SCALE).

DETAIL SHOWING THE "BULK" AN ALTERNATIVE "CRATCH" DECORATION.

SECTION SHOWING RELATIONSHIP OF ENGINE AND BOILER.

C/L ENGINE.

C/L PROPELLOR AND CRANKSHAFT.

SECTION A-A

OUTLINE ELEVATION OF F.M.C STEAMER (NOT TO SCALE).

C.W.R.

FMC Steam Narrow Boat – Key to diagram

1 Towing hook
2 Tunnel hook
3 Engine-room hatch and ventilator
4 Engine-room slide
5 Coal-bunker lids
6 Gang planks
7 Stretcher beams (4 off)
8 Cratch (assembly)
9 Towing stud
10 Anser pin and shackle
11 Displacement lubricator for high-pressure cylinder
12 High-pressure cylinder (valve chest cover)
13 Throttle lever
14 Steam transfer pipe from high- to low-pressure cylinder
15 Low-pressure cylinder (valve chest cover)
16 Reversing lever
17 Stephenson's valve gear
18 Spill pipe
19 Boiler feed pump
20 Tiller and extension
21 Rudder post
22 Skeg
23 Outboard bearing for propeller shaft
24 Screw propeller
25 Spill pipe outlet from boiler feed pump (see 18)
26 Diverter valve assembly
27 Exhaust steam pipe – steam turned overboard when running non-condensing
28 Jet condenser, mud box and associated pipework
29 Funnel
30 Safety valve outlet pipe
31 Whistle
32 Coal bunkers under roof (alongside boiler)
33 Smokebox door
34 Furnace door
35 Stands
36 Water gauge connections for divorced gauges (one either side)
37 Mud doors (5 off)
38 Box mast
39 Safety valve outlet pipe (see 30)
40 Safety valve and trip lever
41 Main steam valve
42 Steam dome
43 Bulk
44 Fore stud
45 Luby and towing mast
46 False cratch ⎫
47 Deck cratch ⎬ Cratch assembly (see 8)

(Birmingham) boat dock formerly belonging to William Clayton & Co. This was to be the birthplace of many FMC steamers during the next twenty-three years.

The definitive FMC steamer, as built around 1900, was of composite construction (iron sides, elm bottom) and fitted with a 'Haines' engine made by FMC themselves. The Cochrane boiler gave way to a small 'Scotch' return-tube one in boats built or reboilered after 1895. A typical engine had cylinders 5in/10in bore × 10in stroke, using steam at 110psig and developing about 11bhp at 160rpm. A large, three-bladed propeller was fitted. The boats could run condensing or non-condensing at will, a feature which did not make for the most efficient use of steam, nor indeed of compounding. They were worked hard, being on the move day and night except when stopped for loading or by a canal stoppage. The average pair of boats would make fifty-two round trips between London and Birmingham in a year. An all-male complement of six was carried, split into two working crews of three who changed places at set points along the canal rather than at set times. Despite this intensive working, the boats were not entirely satisfactory, either mechanically or financially. The use of three bearings on the propeller shafts of earlier craft was a mistake in something as flexible as a narrow boat, and there were numerous breakdowns until one of the bearings was eliminated. There were, too, many cases where boats or boilers were damaged by careless handling. One wonders how many boats were damaged because their single-crank engines chose to stop on centre at the wrong moment, as for example when entering a lock. FMC tried numerous alternatives to steam, but in 1912 settled on the extremely simple and highly reliable Bolinder two-stroke oil engine. Adoption of this legendary power plant spelt the end of steam (and horse) traction as far as FMC were concerned. Not only was it more economical but it occupied only half the space of the steam plant, thus increasing the carrying capacity of the motor boat by 5 tons, and as it did not require a full-time engineer it enabled boat crews to be reduced. But for World War I, it is likely that FMC's steamers would have disappeared before 1920; they were, however, reprieved and ran until 1927. A few lasted even longer in the hands of smaller carriers.

There were some belated attempts to build 'modern' steamers using steam-lorry power plant. One such was the *Sentinel* of 1927, which as its name suggests used the engine and boiler of the famous Sentinel steam wagon. The engine was a single-cylinder unit, half of a standard lorry engine in fact, but even so it was far too big. None of these craft made any impression on the growing number of diesel-engined boats because they could not overcome the dual handicap of a larger engine-room and the need for an extra crew member.

The narrow steam tug had a longer history. Such tugs were used for two distinct purposes, towing boats either for a fairly long distance on a relatively lock-free canal or through tunnels that did not possess a towing path. Once again James Inshaw led the way, when in 1855 he won the £100 prize offered by the Regent's Canal for the most practical steam tug able to haul trains of boats on that waterway. Inshaw's *Birmingham* was a full-length tug of similar layout to his carrying craft mentioned earlier, and though of only 8nhp was capable of hauling trains of barges weighing up to 600 tons. Two more tugs of the same design were purchased by the Regent's Canal and the trio remained in service until 1870.

The only narrow tugs to copy Inshaw's basic layout were those of the Bridgewater Canal. These, though built for a wide canal, were of only 8ft beam and like Inshaw's *Birmingham* had a cabin that resembled those of the earlier canal passenger boats. For this reason they were always known as 'packets'. A fairly large locomotive boiler was mounted just forward of centre, and behind this was a single-cylinder horizontal engine, laid lengthways, which drove the propeller through bevel gearing. The 'packets' remained steam powered until the 1920s, when they were converted to diesel power. Somewhat similar in concept, though less elegant, were the tunnel tugs of the Trent & Mersey Canal, used through Barnton and

Charles Nelson & Co Ltd, cement manufacturers of Stockton, Warwickshire, built three steamers at their own yard in the 1880s. With Cochrane boilers and two-cylinder simple engines, they cannot have differed much in outward appearance from the earlier Grand Junction boats. They normally ran between Stockton and London, but occasionally ventured down the Stratford Canal to Wilmcote, where their neighbours (and fellow steamboat operators) Greaves, Bull & Lakin had limeworks. In this 'action' shot, *Jason* is tied back to the head of a lock, a common artifice in the days of unwieldy cameras and slow emulsions. Note that a water barrel is carried instead of the traditional painted can (*Waterways Museum*)

Preston Brook tunnels. These had spring-loaded wheels mounted over the sides so that they did not have to be steered while passing through the tunnel. They were the last steam tugs in service on a narrow canal when they were withdrawn in 1943.

The Grand Junction Canal built a number of steam tugs to supplement their cargo-carrying 'tugs', but these were not sold when the company gave up commercial carrying. Instead they were used to operate a regular towing service through Braunston and Blisworth tunnels. These services began in 1871 and continued for something over sixty years. The early tugs had engines and boilers similar to those in the carrying fleet, but the boilers proved unable to sustain the effort needed to tow a long train of boats through a restricted channel for forty-five minutes or so and were soon replaced by locomotive-type boilers. The old 'Elliott' engines proved quite satisfactory, however, and frequent rebuilding or replacement in kind kept this type alive into the 1920s. Only then did the company purchase a number of modern tugs with steel hulls and compound engines. By the early 1930s the small number of unpowered craft using the canal no longer

The *Empress* of 1898 was an 'accountant's rebuild' of a boat built in 1887 and besides the name it also used the original engine, probably to give credibility to the 'rebuild'. A new 'Haines' engine of FMC manufacture was fitted in 1899. The top of the high-pressure cylinder projected through the roof of the engine-room on these boats, hence the large box in rear of the funnel. The legend '9437 13¼ TONS' above the name is the registration at Watermans' Hall for operation on tidal reaches of the Thames outside Brentford or Regent's Canal docks. *Empress* was photographed heading south through Berkhamsted with the main line of the London & North Western Railway in the background (*David McDougall, Black Country Museum*)

justified regular tug services.

A number of full-length steam tugs worked long-distance services on the southern end of the Grand Junction Canal. Similar in design to contemporary carrying craft, they were generally family boats and because they had living accommodation were of necessity registered with the local public health authority. Only a handful of tugs were so registered in the whole country, those on the Grand Junction making up most of the number.

19

(*opposite above*)
Vulcan was built in 1906 and at first carried a Crossley suction-gas engine for comparative trials against the existing steamers. This was replaced in 1910 by a steam plant comprising a Ruston Proctor 'Scotch' boiler and a 'Haines' engine built by A. H. Beasley & Sons of Uxbridge. *Vulcan*, too, is seen tied back to the head of a lock, and in this view her engine is exhausting to the condenser, the cooling water being turned overboard below the engine-room doors (*Collection, Alan Faulkner*)

(*opposite centre*)
An FMC steamer approaches the southern portal of Blisworth Tunnel past a short line-up of horse boats waiting for the tunnel tug. The tug itself can be seen in the background, partly hidden by its own exhaust. On the left are the crew room and stores for the tug service (*M. Palmer; Collection, Michael Ware*)

(*left*)
Two FMC steamers were on permanent hire to John Dickinson & Co Ltd around 1920, carrying paper from their Apsley mills to the Port of London. *Countess* and *Princess* were painted in Dickinson's colours for this service, and the former boat is here seen at Bulls Bridge, Hayes, Middlesex. Features of interest include the padded cratch or 'bulk', a purely decorative effect produced by a pair of shaped sideboards and a canvas sheet padded with hay or straw, and a member of the crew posing with a melodion. In pre-radio days this was a favourite instrument among the boat people (*Wm Knibbs; Collection, Alan Faulkner*)

(*above*)
An unidentified FMC steamer towing the butty *Boxmoor* waits to enter Town Lock, Rickmansworth in this early morning study. Unusually, the funnel and cabin chimney have been decorated with brass bands in the manner of a family boat, in contrast to the normal austere appearance of FMC's hard-worked steamers. Note the method of towing with a long line taken over the mast of the butty and back through running blocks to the cabin stud, the original method of towing by horse or motor which allowed the steerer of the butty to pay out the line and take up the load gently (*Collection, Michael Ware*)

The authors of this book gained some first-hand experience of commercial narrow-boat operation with the motor boat *Admiral*, which began its life in 1905 as a Fellows, Morton steamer. The engine and boiler of *Admiral* were, fortunately, photographed as examples of standard practice. The 5ft diameter 'Scotch' boiler came from John Thompson & Co Ltd of Wolverhampton. It had fifty-four tubes of 2¼in outside diameter, of which ten were thick-walled stay tubes. Working pressure was 110psig. This type of boiler was used in all the later FMC steamers (*FMC slide; Collection, C. P. Weaver*)

Admiral was fitted with a 'Haines' engine made by FMC themselves at Saltley. The condenser is mounted on the bedplate, both the condenser air pump and the boiler feed pump being driven by eccentrics on the crankshaft. Adjacent to the low-pressure cylinder is the diverter valve, by means of which the engine could work condensing or non-condensing at will. Slots in the flywheel rim are provided for barring the engine, but had it stopped on centre one feels that the average engineman would have put his foot on one of the spokes to get it started. Stopping on centre must have been a constant problem with this type of

engine and would prove extremely embarassing should it happen when entering a lock (*FMC slide; Collection, C. P. Weaver*)

(*opposite, below left*)
The last few FMC steamers had 'Haines' engines made by A. H. Beasley & Sons of Rockingham Ironworks, Uxbridge. These were similar to the Saltley product but were built up on four columns and had the pumps driven from the crossheads through rocking beams, more in the manner of a marine engine. Beasley's engines had slightly smaller cylinders and worked at a higher pressure than their predecessors. *Viceroy* worked the last commercial trip by a steamer in FMC colours, from City Road Basin to Uxbridge, in November 1927 (*Waterways Museum*)

(*top*)
Photographed at Stoke Bruerne, the wooden-hulled tunnel tug *Spider* was built in 1870 and lasted until 1928. It had a small locomotive-type boiler supplied by Davey Paxman of Colchester, and a single-cylinder 10hp 'Elliott' engine made in the Grand Junction's own City Road works. The raked stem may have been provided to facilitate ice-breaking, though this was a risky procedure with a wooden boat. The unusual curved tiller appears on other tugs of the period and may have been inherited from early commercial craft (*Waterways Museum*)

(*above*)
In 1922 the GJCC replaced the tunnel tug *Hasty*, built in 1896, with a new vessel of the same name from Bushell Bros of Tring. The new tug is seen moored in the old Wendover Arm shortly after being launched from Bushell's yard. It had a loco-motive boiler, again by Davey Paxman, and a two-cylinder compound engine by Beasley (*Institute of Agricultural History and Museum of English Rural Life, University of Reading*)

23

The Eastern Counties Navigation & Transport Co Ltd was formed in 1889 with the object of reopening the River Larke Navigation to Bury St Edmunds. In 1889 they bought four narrow tugs from Edward Hayes of Watling Works, Stony Stratford, another noted builder of small steam boats. These were generally similar to the contemporary GJCC tugs but had machinery designed and built by Hayes himself. Tug No 3 *The Bury St Edmunds* has just arrived at Bury St Edmunds in this photograph dated October 1892, which doubtless shows the arrival of the first commercial traffic since completion of the restoration works. The craft used were of course fen lighters and the photograph shows the way in which these were coupled together in a train so that individual boats did not have to be steered. Despite the high hopes entertained by the top-hatted gentlemen who have gathered to watch this event, the navigation was again derelict by 1904 (*W. A. Spanton, Suffolk County Council; Collection, Alan Faulkner*)

The Trent & Mersey Canal had a number of narrow tugs that worked through Barnton and Preston Brook tunnels. They were similar to the Bridgewater Canal tugs but characterised by a pair of outriggers on either side that carried spring-loaded wheels, these wheels ran along the sides of the tunnel and obviated the need to steer the boat, at the same time protecting the tunnel structure from unnecessary wear and tear. This photograph purports to be taken on the canal at Barnton, but it is obviously taken on a fairly wide river and must therefore be on the River Weaver, probably between Weston Point and Anderton. It is suggested that the tugs were being used to work traffic round a stoppage on the canal itself by way of the River Weaver and the Anderton boat lift (*Rugby Portland Cement; Collection, Alan Faulkner*)

(*opposite above*)

This view of the Grand Union Canal at Hatton was taken in 1934 after completion of the widening between Braunston and Birmingham. The old narrow locks can be seen on the right of the new flight and there are piles of old lock gates on either side of the canal. Tied up opposite the maintenance depot between the fourth and fifth locks of the Hatton flight is the ex-GJCC steam tug *de Salis*, built by Bushell Bros in 1923 to the same general specification as *Hasty*. Displaced from tunnel duties by the almost total disappearance of horse boats, it is being used for maintenance work. Alongside the depot are two boats carrying the component parts of a steam piling rig used to drive piles for bank protection (*Waterways Museum*)

(*opposite centre*)

Bushell Bros built quite a few steam tugs in their yard adjacent to New Mills, Tring. The yard originally belonged to William Mead & Co, flour millers, and was managed by John Bushell; in 1875 it became an independent concern and lasted until 1952. In this photograph, taken in 1906, the full-length tug *Buffalo* has just undergone a major refit and the semi-wide boat *Osprey* is nearing completion in the background. Both craft belong to Wm Mead. *Buffalo* was built at Uxbridge in 1890 for the short-lived London/Birmingham Canal Carrying Company, and when that failed was purchased by Mead to haul trains of wide boats like *Osprey* between the Port of London

and the mills at Tring. Having been built for long-distance work, the tug has two cabins of which the front one is a proper living cabin, and it is therefore registered with the local public health authority under the terms of the Canal Boats Act (*Institute of Agricultural History and Museum of English Rural Life, University of Reading*)

(*opposite below*)

Antelope was another full-length tug and a sister to *Buffalo*, having the same history. It is seen here in July 1911 near Alperton on the lower Grand Junction Canal hauling a train of semi-wide (11ft beam) boats towards Tring. The loaded ones are carrying corn, the empty ones are used only to carry flour in the opposite direction. Though fitted with comparatively small engines, these tugs could move a large tonnage in a deep, wide waterway (*Hertford County Records Office, Stingemore Collection*)

(*above*)

Charrington Gardner Locket & Co Ltd, the large London coal merchants, were another user of full-length narrow tugs with living accommodation; these were unusual in being family boats. In this view taken near Kensal Green, one of their tugs is approaching the gasworks with a train of at least three wide boats loaded with gas coal. Note the additional supply of steam coal stacked behind the funnel (*Express Newspapers; Collection, C. P. Weaver*)

Wide Canal Craft

The earliest reference to steam craft on an *inland* wide canal, as opposed to a ship canal, is in the mid-1820s when the committee of the Nottingham Canal banned steamboats on the familiar grounds of bank erosion. The Thames & Severn Canal, on the other hand, took a more enlightened view and followed with interest the experiments of David Gordon and John McCurdy. When McCurdy's first trip to Oxford proved unsuccessful, John Denyer, the Thames & Severn manager, commented that it was a pity as it might discourage others from trying. Despite this enlightened attitude, however, no regular steam services ever operated over that singularly unfortunate waterway.

The first purpose-built canal steamers were built by the Aire & Calder Navigation in 1853. They were of fairly advanced design, having a compact and efficient power plant mounted right aft so that it occupied the minimum amount of space. The plant comprised a small multi-tubular boiler, either vertical or locomotive type, and a two-cylinder simple expansion 'inverted diagonal' engine. In modern parlance this meant a V-twin, and that type of engine was to become very popular on northern waterways. With cylinders at 90 degrees, it has the same characteristics as a two-crank engine but occupies no more than half the space (ie, length of hull) and has somewhat superior balance. These early Aire & Calder boats were an instant success; operating mainly at night in the absence of other traffic they were capable of maintaining an overall average speed of 4½mph, but unlike most of their successors they did not tow additional boats.

Ten years later the Aire & Calder took a major step forward with the introduction of the compartment-boat system devised and patented by their engineer, W. H. Bartholomew, in 1862. As originally executed, this was the first commercial application of the pusher tug, an idea first mooted by Edwin Thomas of the Regent's Canal in 1859. The heart of the system was the rectangular compartment boat, or 'Tom Pudding', six of which were sandwiched between a short steam tug at the rear and a false bow or *jebus* at the front. Each unit of the train could pivot about the stem post of the unit behind, and by tightening or

slackening the cables which ran along each side of the train it could be steered with fair precision. On arrival at the port of Goole, the compartments were lifted bodily and tipped directly into the holds of waiting ships by special hoists, also designed by Bartholomew.

Prototype trains were ordered from the firm of Hudswell & Clarke (predecessors of Hudswell Clarke & Co) in 1862. The earliest tugs had the same inverted diagonal engines as the commercial boats, supplied with steam by small locomotive-type boilers. After extensive trials, more equipment was obtained and the full service started in 1864. By the 1890s traffic had outgrown the short trains originally envisaged and there was a gradual change to conventional towing, by which means up to nineteen compartments could be handled at a time. The change-over was not complete until 1904, yet surprisingly no photograph of an original Bartholomew train with pusher tug is known to exist. Given the enthusiasm for photography, and cine photography, in late Victorian Yorkshire, this is both disappointing and amazing.

With the change to conventional towing, newer compartment tugs were equipped with larger engines, usually two-cylinder compounds made by Earle's of Hull, and had 'Scotch' boilers from the same builder. Steam towage lasted into the 1950s and not until 1956 was the first tug converted to diesel power.

The adjoining Leeds & Liverpool Canal did not make any serious use of steam power until 1880. It then commissioned the Wigan firm of George Wilkinson & Co to design a self-propelled commercial boat capable of towing one or two additional boats. Probably starting from the well-tried Aire & Calder designs, Wilkinson tried out a number of different engine and boiler configurations before arriving at a satisfactory layout. This comprised a vertical Field-tube boiler and a four-cylinder compound version of the well-tried inverted diagonal engine, each arm of the 'V' being a tandem compound unit. The Field tube is a thimble projecting downwards from the firebox crown of an otherwise conventional vertical boiler. Inside the thimble is a smaller tube which acts as a down-comer, promoting vigorous circulation of water in the thimble and on the adjacent areas of crownsheet. It produces a simple, fast-steaming boiler within a comparatively small envelope.

These Leeds & Liverpool boats were a great success and the company eventually operated a sizeable fleet of them. They were, like most pure canal craft, non-condensing and therefore their compound engines did not really justify themselves unless worked at full power, as when towing additional craft. Some later boats were, therefore, provided with plain simple-expansion engines because they would normally work alone. Many Leeds & Liverpool boats ended their days in the hands of private traders, and they could still be seen on the canal until the early 1950s.

There was but one attempt to build a wide steamer on the Grand Junction Canal. Although the locks are 14ft wide, this is not a true wide canal because 14ft boats cannot pass one another at many places along the canal due to the restricted cross-section of the main channel. A special semi-wide boat was therefore developed for use on the southern end of the canal, a boat similar in appearance to a narrow boat but 11ft wide, tapering to 7ft wide at the bottom. This was the largest boat that could pass another of its kind anywhere on the canal. Ever on the look out for something better than a steam narrow boat, Fellows, Morton & Clayton had one steam semi-wide boat built for comparison, the *Swan* of 1911.

Swan had an oil-fired, water-tube boiler and a two-cylinder compound engine of 4in/8in bore × 5in stroke that developed 45bhp at 600rpm, both made by T. & A. Savery of Newcomen Street, Birmingham. The idea of installing so much power was that *Swan* could work down the Thames from Brentford towing one or two dumb barges; on the canal it would work singly, transhipping its cargo to narrow boats at Braunston, the northern limit of wide locks. Presumably the ability to work down-river and a reduction in crew from six to four were expected to outweigh the disadvantage of having to tranship the cargo. On trial on the Thames, *Swan* hauled a 45-ton barge at 4.86mph, but on the canal her engine must surely have been too big and too fast for efficient operation. Between August 1911 and January

1912 she made twenty-five round trips between Brentford and Braunston, taking 90 hours (net) for each round trip. It was not a successful experiment. *Swan* carried only 34 tons, less than a pair of narrow boats, far less than the 50 tons of an unpowered semi-wide boat. The steam plant was, if anything, more of a handicap than it was in a narrow boat and the experiment was not repeated.

We have chosen to end this section by taking a look at an aspect of 'steam on the canals' which rarely receives due recognition. It is well known that in the heyday of the steamship, British yards built the merchant fleets of most countries in the world. Less well known is the fact that British yards also built many of the launches and cargo steamers that plied the world's rivers and lakes. (How

many tourists aboard the Mississippi stern-wheeler *Delta Queen* realise that she was built on the Clyde?) Several yards whose products found their way to remote parts of all five continents were located on inland waterways, like the Watling Works of Edward Hayes at Stony Stratford. Brimscombe canal port on the Thames & Severn Canal was the site chosen by Edwin Clarke to start a boatyard in 1878, and after his death in 1895 it became part of Isaac J. Abdela & Mitchell Ltd. Clarke was a pioneer of galvanised steel hulls and like many small yards built a range of standardised sectional river steamers. Abdela Mitchell continued and developed this work. Everything built at Brimscombe was launched into the basin for steam and stability trials. Some launches then went through the canal to Sharpness or perhaps London (when the Thames & Severn was open) for shipment. Larger craft were dismantled for shipment and might not be reassembled until they had travelled half-way round the world. (Enthusiasts will enjoy Werner Herzog's *Fitzcarraldo*, filmed in Peru and featuring British-made vessels of this kind). The photographs of Brimscombe-built craft that survive are not only a valuable record of a vanished industry but are also among the few illustrations of the Thames & Severn Canal as an operational waterway. We make no apologies for including a number of them in this book.

The Aire & Calder Navigation was an early user of powered carrying craft capable of towing one or more dumb craft. Merchandise Tug No 12 is typical of later vessels in this category, which, despite a cabin and engine-room taking up half their length, still had a useful capacity of 30 tons. It was built in 1875 and is photographed at Goole around the turn of the century, lying outside the swing bridge between the Ship and Ouse docks. This side view emphasises the height of the dome on the locomotive-type boiler fitted to these boats and also shows the counterweighted arms which extend below the chimney hinge so that it can be lowered by one man (*British Waterways Board*)

An overhead view of a merchandise tug shows the deck layout, which was dominated by the tall dome and funnel. Note the twin Salter safety valves and pressure gauge, the latter being provided for the benefit of the engineman when he was on deck. Controls are provided on deck so that the engine can be driven by the steerer or by the engineman. The massive samson post was used when towing other craft, the cabin chimney being removed in such cases. Up front is the white-painted mast, which carried a large headlight during the hours of darkness and also served as a useful marker when running empty with the bows high out of the water (*British Waterways Board*)

Unique to the Aire & Calder was the Bartholomew compartment-boat system. In this relatively modern view, Compartment Tug No 14 is returning from Goole to the South Yorkshire coalfield with a standard train of nineteen boats. The *jebus* is attached to the tug when hauling an empty train; on a loaded train it goes on the leading compartment to reduce head-end resistance (*British Waterways Board*)

Compartment Tug No 13 was built in 1880 and is typical of the short, rather dumpy tugs used in the days of push-towage. It had a power plant generally similar to that fitted in the merchandise tugs. By the time this photograph was taken at Goole in 1908, pushing had ceased and most of the tugs had lost the rams by which the original trains had been steered. Note the stern of an Aire & Calder river tug on the right and the dismantled steam crane on the wharf. The latter looks like a product of one of the Leeds builders (*British Waterways Board*)

(*opposite above*)
A slightly earlier photograph of Compartment Tug No 10 shows the large hydraulic rams mounted on deck for steering a pushed train of compartment boats. Most of the associated equipment has been removed, however. The bluff bows of these early tugs fitted into a matching stern on the first compartment boat and contact between other members of the train was achieved in the same way, the unit in front pivoting about the stem of the one behind. Of particular interest in this picture is a rare view of a *jebus* from the rear. This device took its name from the Latin *gibbus*, a hump (*British Waterways Board*)

(*opposite below*)
On arrival at Goole, compartment boats were tipped bodily into the holds of waiting ships by special hydraulically powered hoists, two of which are seen in this 1953 view of the South Dock. On the right is one of four fixed hoists, while in the foreground two compartment tugs are bringing the unique No 4 floating hoist out of No 2 dry-dock, on completion of its first overhaul since being built in 1908. No 4 hoist could be moved about the docks to provide extra capacity wherever it was required (*Waterways Museum*)

An unusual form of propulsion tried out on the Aire & Calder in 1867 was the cable traction system developed by John Fowler & Co of Leeds. A modified portable engine of 4nhp was equipped with a clip drum by means of which it hauled itself along a wire rope laid at the side of the canal. This particular form of cable tug was developed for the American market, several being supplied to the Delaware & Hudson Canal, and it is one of these units that featured in the trials. By using a portable engine, there was no need for a separate tug, the engine being changed from boat to boat as required. Second from the left in the group aboard the boat is Max Eyth (1836–1906), a mainstay of the Fowler organisation from 1861 until 1882 and one of Europe's leading authorities on agricultural machinery and cable traction. Fourth from the left is Robert Burton, who in 1858 invented the clip drum used on all Fowler cable tugs. The rim of the drum consists of a series of pivoted jaws which grip the cable tightly by the action of its own tension, thus enabling a half-turn round the drum to provide all the grip necessary for the hardest job (*Institute of Agricultural History and Museum of English Rural Life, University of Reading*)

(*opposite above*)
In this period study of organised leisure, three Leeds & Liverpool steamers are trapped in the ice at the top of the famous Bingley Five-rise. Like their counterparts elsewhere, these boats were intended to haul additional craft when necessary and were therefore provided with a towing hook at the top of the rudder post, so that the towing line did not pass inboard of the tiller (*Waterways Museum*)

(*opposite below*)
Another photograph taken at Bingley – apparently a favourite location of contemporary photographers – shows one of the Leeds & Liverpool full-length tugs. These were used for all sorts of duties, including regular towage service through Gannow and Foulridge tunnels and, in winter, ice-breaking. They were similar in mechanical specification to the carrying craft. It is recorded that in this photograph of No 57 the crew comprises James Gore (Captain), Robert Varley, Jack Spencer and Ernest Wheatley. How one wishes that all photographers recorded such details for posterity! (*Craven Museum; Collection, G. Biddle*)

The inverted diagonal engine was widely used on northern waterways and engines of this type powered most of the Leeds & Liverpool fleet. The original engines made by George Wilkinson were four-cylinder, non-condensing compounds, but because a compound engine has to work hard to show any gain over a simple when no condenser is fitted, some of the later steamers were equipped with simple engines only. Steam was normally supplied by a vertical boiler, the base of which can just be seen at the top of this photograph. The unusual amount of space in this engine-room suggests that it belongs to a tug, for on a commercial boat the boiler would have been much closer to the engine to save space (*Waterways Museum*)

At least one Leeds & Liverpool steamer had a vertical tandem compound engine like those on Fellows, Morton narrow boats. It appears to have been assembled from standard parts by a builder of small marine engines, and unusually for a canal boat engine it has Hackworth valve gear. The spaciousness of this engine-room suggests that it, too, belongs to a tug (*Waterways Museum*)

(*top*)
The semi-wide boat *Swan* was the last Fellows, Morton & Clayton experiment with steam power. Measuring 70ft × 11ft, *Swan* was the largest boat capable of working regularly on the Grand Junction Canal and could carry 34 tons. Having been designed to tow dumb barges on the Thames, she was far too powerful for efficient operation on the canal as a single boat. The only obvious advantage was that it could be worked by two men instead of the three required for a steam narrow boat and butty (*Arthur Newton; Collection, Alan Faulkner*)

The last five photographs in this section pay tribute to one of the small boatyards that sent British-built steam launches to the lakes and rivers of five continents. Edwin Clarke established his yard at Brimscombe on the Thames & Severn Canal in 1878 and became one of the pioneers of galvanised steel construction. On his death in 1895 the yard became part of Isaac J. Abdela & Mitchell Ltd which continued the Clarke tradition. This photograph of the launch *Mimi*, with Isaac Abdela at the wheel, was taken in the canal basin at Brimscombe against the background of the elegant warehouse (*Air Plants Ltd*)

(*opposite above*)
S. Raymundo is a classic Abdela & Mitchell launch with boiler and engine made on the premises. Note the clean lines and economy of design, a hallmark of the yard. Note too the large return-tube boiler, fitted to ensure adequate steam-raising capacity even when burning poor fuel. This would be a necessary feature in a boat destined to spend its life on a remote and probably treacherous river. *S. Raymundo* probably went to South America, and may well have begun its journey by canal under its own power (*Air Plants Ltd*)

(*opposite centre*)
Photographs of Abdela Mitchell craft are among the few surviving illustrations of the Thames & Severn Canal as an active waterway. Observe the absence of water-weed and the immaculate condition of the banks and towpath in the view of another standard launch, the *Torpedera*. This, too, was probably destined for South America, which was an important market in the days when British finance controlled much of that continent's industry and communications (*Air Plants Ltd*)

(*opposite below*)
The largest vessels ever to float on an inland canal in this country were probably the Abdela Mitchell *Islandia* class of sectional river steamers. *Islandia* herself went to a tributary of the Amazon in northern Peru; *Asturiana* is a slightly smaller vessel which from its name could be destined for Spain or South America. Note the steering position well forward on the upper deck, a typical Brimscombe feature, and the two large air vents alongside the funnel which may indicate that the boiler (on the lower deck) has a closed stokehold (*Air Plants Ltd*)

(*above*)
On 12 December 1912 the Cardiff Watch Committee inspected their new fire float *Fire Queen*, another product of Abdela Mitchell's yard. This photograph, taken on the Glamorganshire Canal near the City Hall, is almost certainly of that event, as the two figures prominent in the centre of the picture are Isaac J. Abdela and Superintendent G. Geen of the Cardiff Fire Brigade. *Fire Queen* was apparently ordered from Merryweather & Sons, and must therefore have been a joint effort, Abdela Mitchell building the boat (and probably the propelling machinery) while Merryweather supplied the special oil-fired pumping unit and associated equipment. The fire pump would be similar to that used on their self-propelled steam fire engines, a small boiler being kept in steam continuously to warm the oil so that the main boiler could be lit up at a moment's notice and the engine be running at full power within ten minutes; a man kept watch on board at all times. *Fire Queen* was normally kept in the Timber Pond, near Dunballs Road, in telephonic communication with the main fire station; from here she could proceed on to the canal and thus through the heart of the city or out into the Bute West Dock and gain access to the 165 acres of enclosed water. The boat was commissioned early in 1913 and served until October 1935; being then sold to a Swansea firm. While being towed there she ran aground on the Tusker Rock, off Porthcawl, and her ultimate fate is unknown (*Welsh Industrial & Maritime Museum*)

Rivers and Ship Canals

The Forth & Clyde Canal is an appropriate introduction to this chapter because it was a ship canal of a rather unusual kind. Too small to be of much use to conventional shipping, it justified the description by developing two classes of seagoing canal boats, one of which was to become a famous coaster in its own right. The idea of making canal boats that were sufficiently seaworthy to venture out on to the Forth and Clyde estuaries went back to the *Cyclops* of 1830 (see Chapter 1), but it was not until 1856 that the canal committee agreed to the development of steam-powered commercial craft. Their first effort was the steam scow *Thomas* which went into service in September 1856. This was an 80-ton boat powered by a two-cylinder simple engine of 6¼in bore × 10in stroke, its large vertical multi-tubular boiler being designed to work at 100psig. *Thomas* was intended to tow two dumb scows, but it was soon found that the disadvantages of towing extra craft outweighed the advantages. So in practice *Thomas* worked singly and its boiler was never pressed beyond 40psig; it was over-powered in this role.

In 1858 a two-cylinder engine of even greater dimensions, 9½in bore × 15in stroke, was fitted to the company's ice-breaker/dredger, and a second engine of

The earliest steam carrying craft on the Forth & Clyde Canal were steam-powered versions of the traditional 'scow' used on the canal since its opening. The vessel took its name from the Dutch word for a flat-bottomed boat, and was quite unsuited to operation on tidal waters. A steam scow was equipped with a small, simple-expansion engine and an equally compact vertical boiler, being of course non-condensing for simplicity. Depending upon the density of canal traffic, the average steam scow could carry a load of 60–80 tons at 2½–4mph. This photograph shows Carron Iron Works No 16 heading towards Carron with a load of iron ore from the company's workings at Cadder. Note how the loose cargo is restrained by detachable sideboards (*G. Langmuir*)

similar size was used for a 120-ton seagoing lighter in 1860. From these prototypes were developed three long-lasting classes of steamer. The simplest was the steam scow, capable only of working on the canal and based on *Thomas*. The first of these was *James*, launched in August 1859 and fitted with a single-cylinder engine of 7in bore × 9in stroke working at 75psig. Next in importance was an approximately 80-ton version of the seagoing lighter. These had engines not much larger than that fitted to *James* but rather larger boilers; being non-condensing, they soon acquired the name 'Puffer'. This type was soon improved by the addition of bulwarks so that they could operate in the open sea, thus creating the true Scottish 'Puffer' which was for so long an integral part of the Highland transport scene. With the advent of the seagoing Puffer, the earlier seagoing lighter acquired the unofficial name 'Inside Puffer'. The history of the Puffer belongs mainly to the realm of coastal shipping, but they continued to be a familiar sight on the Forth & Clyde Canal until its closure in 1962. Many Puffers were built in yards on the banks of the canal, such as J. & J. Hay and Peter MacGregor, both of Kirkintilloch.

Steamboats generally similar to the Forth & Clyde scows were to be found on some of the smaller English rivers, but in general river traffic was handled either by tugs towing existing horse- or sail-powered craft or by small coasters similar to the Puffers. A notable design in the latter category was the steam 'flat' found on the River Weaver and used by such large concerns as Brunner Mond to convey their products to Liverpool and other points on the Mersey Estuary. From these it was but a small step to the true steam coaster which could be seen on the estuaries of most large rivers and making use of associated waterways such as the Gloucester & Berkeley Canal. Such craft were similar in design to contemporary deep-sea shipping, as far as their propulsive machinery was concerned.

Tugs employed on rivers and ship canals were usually small versions of contemporary harbour tugs, though there were occasional variations such as the *Little John* of the Trent Navigation Co. Paddle tugs were rarely seen except in the early days, with the notable exception of the fleet operated by the Manchester Ship Canal until the early 1950s. It is only in quite recent times that screw tugs have been able to match the low-speed power and manoeuvrability of a similarly sized paddle tug with an independent engine for each wheel, hence the retention of a small number of such tugs by the MSC for controlling the stern of a large, empty vessel during its passage down the canal.

The Manchester Ship Canal is our only really large ship canal, and over the years has been host to virtually every type of seagoing steamship apart from the very largest. To represent this side of our story, we have chosen to depict the various types of steamer that gathered for the opening of the canal in 1894. Despite the presence of Queen Victoria, the Royal Yacht was not in attendance; the substitute Admiralty Yacht *Enchantress* is, however, of more interest.

To close this section, mention must be made of the quadruple-screw tug *Wagtail*, built by J. H. Wilson & Co of Liverpool in 1875. It was designed by a local marine architect, St Clare Byrne, for service on the River Weaver and was a true shallow-draught tug, a type rarely used on a British waterway. In principle it was identical with a Mississippi stern-wheeler, having a shallow flat-bottomed hull with swim ends so that water had a free passage under rather than round the hull. Four screws were used to compensate for the shallow draught, thus achieving maximum blade area relative to the cross-section of the hull. The screws were protected from damage by sideplates that were in fact an extension of the hull sheathing. *Wagtail* was probably the last tug to be designed with the classic Inshaw layout of longitudinal engines driving through bevel gears. Each pair of screws could be run independently, but except when manoeuvring they would have been clutched together to eliminate any tendency to asymmetric thrust. Sadly no details have survived by which to assess the success or otherwise of this unusual design, but as it does not seem to have been repeated one must assume that it showed no real advantage over a conven-tional tug. Coincidentally, St Clare Byrne designed the yacht which headed the procession at the opening of the Manchester Ship Canal in 1894.

(*opposite above*)

A direct development of the steam scow was the 'Inside Puffer', a more seaworthy vessel capable of venturing on to the estuaries at either end of the canal. Inside Puffers had the same rather simple machinery as scows, though of somewhat greater power in view of their operation in more demanding waters. This turn of the century view shows two Inside Puffers tied up alongside the boatyard of J. &. J. Hay Ltd, Kirkintilloch, a leading builder and operator of such craft. Many Inside Puffers were worked extremely hard, making up to five round trips between Glasgow and Grangemouth in a week. They disappeared in the 1920s with the decline in local canal traffic (*Strathkelvin Libraries*)

(*opposite below*)

The final development of the Forth & Clyde steamer was the legendary 'Puffer', a true coastal steamer capable of operating through the canal and of being beached for unloading at remote communities in the Highlands and Islands. Like their immediate predecessors, the early Puffers were non-condensing, probably the last non-condensing deep-sea craft to be built. Despite the early adoption of condensers, however, the original name stuck. This photograph shows *Gael*, built by J. &. J. Hay Ltd of Kirkintilloch in 1931, passing Craigmarloch lift bridge with a load of Baltic timber for Brownlee & Co of Glasgow (*J. Watson*)

(*above*)

Representative of the small harbour tugs that worked the lower reaches of major rivers such as the Trent is the United Towing Company's *Riverman*, built in Holland in 1915 and seen collecting a tow of empty Trent boats bound for Hull. Its owners were based in Hull and operated a number of similar craft on the Humber estuary and associated waterways. In the background is the Keadby lift bridge on the main line of the Great Central Railway from South Yorkshire to their own port of Immingham (*Gainsborough Library*)

(opposite above)
On the higher reaches of the River Trent, towage was in the hands of the Trent Navigation Company, whose tug *Little John* is here passing Newark Castle on the approach to Town Lock with a string of loaded Trent boats bound for Nottingham. All of the company's tugs carried names associated with Robin Hood, *Little John* having been built by Yarrow & Co of Glasgow. Designed to operate in shallow water, it drew only 22in of water and was propelled by twin screws working in tunnels and provided with Yarrow's Patent Balanced Hinged Flaps. The screws were driven through gearing from a single two-cylinder simple engine. In this photograph, taken prior to 1920, *Little John* has a large locomotive boiler mounted in the fore end. A Yarrow advertisement of 1922 shows the same vessel with a smaller boiler mounted below a proper fore-deck; whether this was its original or rebuilt form is not clear (*Waterways Museum*)

(opposite below)
Cambridge was for many years an important inland port, a focal point for fen lighters which carried so much of the local traffic in the Fens and adjoining districts until the advent of reliable motor transport in the 1920s. This view of Quayside, Cambridge, was taken around 1900 and shows two steam vessels belonging to the short-lived Eastern Counties Navigation & Transport Co. In the rear is one of their narrow tugs built for operation on the River Larke (see plate 27), with a fen lighter carrying beer casks from the Anchor Brewery, doubtless for distribution to remote Fenland hostelries. In the foreground is the 70-ton steam barge *Nancy*, believed to have been a product of the famous Thetford works of Charles Burrell & Sons Ltd. *Nancy*

operated between Cambridge and King's Lynn until 1914, when she was laid up. Some years later she was towed away for scrap but was instead buried under dredgings on the outskirts of Ely. As this caption was being written, news was received that her remains had been uncovered during excavations for a new marina (*Cambridge & County Folk Museum; Collection, Alan Faulkner*)

(above)
The Great Ouse was once navigable for 72½ miles from King's Lynn to Bedford. In 1893 the moribund upper Ouse was purchased by Leonard Simpson who spent a considerable sum on its restoration and set up the Ouse Transport Co to promote water transport between King's Lynn and Bedford. Frederick Howard, a partner in the famous firm of James & Frederick Howard, was a staunch supporter of the scheme, and as soon as restoration was complete he obtained supplies of pig iron from Yorkshire by way of King's Lynn, the first train of ten lighters arriving at Bedford on 25 July 1895. This photograph shows the train tied up alongside Howard's works shortly after arrival. Simpson's plans were thwarted by opposition from local authorities on the subjects of flood control and the charging of tolls, and he was forced to close the navigation above Holywell on 1 October 1897. J. & F. Howard were for many years one of the world's leading manufacturers of agricultural machinery, also dealing in portable railways as this photograph shows. The firm was a constituent of the ill-fated Agricultural & General Engineers combine in the late 1920s and, like Burrell's of Thetford, was a victim of its eventual collapse on the eve of the Depression (*Collection, Alan Faulkner*)

45

(*opposite above*)
The Ipswich & Stowmarket Navigation, otherwise the River Gipping, was typical of many small waterways. Never particularly busy, it had lost most of its traffic by 1900 and survived for another thirty or so years mainly because of traffic to and from a few large concerns. In this instance the surviving traffic was generated by the Bamford fertilizer and sulphuric acid works operated by E. Packard & Co Ltd, Joseph Fison and Chapman. Packard's works was situated immediately upstream of the bridge carrying the main line of the former Great Eastern Railway and served by Packard's own fleet of four steam barges and thirteen lighters. This view of the works taken around 1920 shows two of the steamers: on the left is *Trent River*, about to go astern and pull a loaded boat out of the covered dock, while that on the right is believed to be *Mersey*. Note the early steam crane with umbrella-like canopy, the variety of crane power outside the works itself and also the characteristic GER signal in the background. Packard, Fison and Prentice Bros (of Stowmarket) amalgamated in 1929, the firm of Fison, Packard & Prentice becoming Fisons Ltd in 1942. The Bramford works is still in production today (*Fisons; Collection, Alan Faulkner*)

(*above*)
Packard's *Trent River* was built by W. H. Orvis & Co of Ipswich in 1916. It measured 51ft 6in × 14ft and could carry 23 tons on a draught of 4ft. The vertical firetube boiler was made by Farrar & Co of Newark and the two-cylinder compound engine (5¼in/10in × 6in) by Plenty & Sons Ltd, Newbury. She is seen heading towards the works having just passed through Bramford lock. On the island in the background can be seen a primitive hand-operated piling frame, a piece of equipment little changed from that used by Roman engineers, yet still found in most waterway maintenance departments until comparatively recent times. River traffic ceased in 1934 and *Trent River* was then bought by her former captain and used to carry shingle from Felixstowe to Ipswich (*Suffolk Records Office; Collection, Alan Faulkner*)

(*opposite centre*)
The end of an era is marked by a special 'run-past' of Severn & Canal Carrying Co tugs at Gloucester in 1931. The line is headed by the new motor tugs *Enterprise* and *Progress*, built by Watson's of Gainsborough in 1929 and 1931 respectively. They are followed by the three remaining SCC steam tugs *Victor*, *Active* and *Alert*. The first two were built at Bristol in 1904 but had only come into SCC ownership in 1926 and were the last steam tugs operated by the company, *Alert* being withdrawn shortly after this photograph was taken. Note that the tugs have no permanent wheelhouse, merely a framework on which canvas sheets can be rigged to give some protection in bad weather. For tugs working on a river, visibility was considered more important than creature comforts! Immediately above *Enterprise* can be seen the ornate chimney of the dock pumping station, which at this time housed two Cornish boilers and Gwynne centrifugal pumps driven by horizontal engines, lifting water from the river into the ship canal. When they were replaced by electric pumps in the mid-1960s, the chimney was demolished (*Waterways Museum*)

(*opposite below*)
The last steam vessel to trade on the Gloucester & Berkeley Canal was F. T. Everard's *Candourity*, seen discharging oil at Quedgeley in March 1967. She was one of many small coastal and estuarine tankers which traded between South Wales and Quedgeley until superseded by a pipeline. She was built by W. J. Yarwood & Sons Ltd of Northwich in 1946 for the Admiralty Naval Stores Department, carrying the number C 641. Everard purchased her in 1956, and two years later lengthened her and converted her to a tanker, at the same time modifying the bridge so that she could pass under the Thames bridges in London. *Candourity* was withdrawn in 1969 and broken up by van den Bossche, of Antwerp. She had a 385ihp triple-expansion engine made by Yarwood and supplied with steam by an oil-fired 'Scotch' boiler. Having the machinery aft, this type of vessel was well suited to carry oil (*C. P. Weaver*)

The quadruple-screw, shallow-draught tug *Wagtail* was built by J. H. Wilson & Co of Liverpool in 1875 for service on the River Weaver. It was a remarkable blend of ancient and futuristic. The actual layout of the machinery was clearly derived from the early twin-screw vessels made by James Inshaw from 1845 onwards, yet the concept of a wide, shallow hull propelled by multiple screws belong to the twentieth century. Outstanding modern examples of the type are those which propel huge trains of barges on the Mississippi, successors to the legendary stern-wheel tugs which achieved the same result by rather different means (*The Engineer*)

(opposite above)
Tied up at Acton Bridge on the River Weaver is the ICI steam packet *Syria*, an 89ft iron steamer dating from 1885. She was built by Joseph Verdin & Son, Winsford, and was at first operated by them, passing to the Salt Union in 1892. She came into ICI ownership in 1943, and four years after this photograph was taken in 1957 was sold to Richard Abel & Sons Ltd of Liverpool. She was broken up in 1967. *Syria* carried about 170 tons and was powered by a two-cylinder simple-expansion engine of 18nhp, 9½in bore × 12in stroke, made by W. E. Baker of Leftwich Dock-yard, Northwich. The vertical return-tube boiler was made by Verdin themselves and installed with the funnel offset to leave a clear view forward from the wheel-house, a feature of all these small packets on the Weaver. Acton Bridge, four miles downstream from Anderton, is the largest on the river and of unusual design. It was designed by

Col J. A. Saner and completed in 1933, but because the area is subject to subsidence (caused by brine pumping), a conventional swing bridge was considered unsuitable. Col Saner therefore floated the main span on a 40ft diameter pontoon, not only combating subsidence but also reducing the effort needed to swing the span. The principle was subsequently adopted elsewhere on the river (*C. P. Weaver*)

(opposite below)
The larger type of steam packet to be found on the River Weaver is represented by the *Davenham*, last steamer to be built for ICI and one of the last two to operate under their colours. *Davenham* was built by W. J. Yarwood & Sons Ltd of Northwich in 1946, powered by a two-cylinder compound engine of 215ihp (12in/26in × 18in) of their own manufacture. Steam at 150psig came from a boiler made by Alex Anderson & Sons Ltd. The boat was 102ft 9in long × 22ft beam and had a carrying capacity of about 260 tons. *Davenham* and *Barnton* were the last steam packets operated by ICI, being sold to the Liverpool Lighterage Co Ltd in 1966; in the crazy world of transport economics it is today considered more efficient to use seven or eight maximum-size lorries to carry the load once taken by a vessel like *Davenham*. In the background of this photograph, taken in the mid-1950s, is the Anderton Boat Lift, joining the Weaver with the Trent & Mersey Canal some 50ft above it. The lift was built in 1875–6 and rebuilt to its present form with independent, counterbalanced caissons in 1906–8 (*ICI*)

The Manchester Ship Canal opened for traffic on 1 January 1894, the official opening by Queen Victoria taking place on Monday 21 May 1894. The former event was marked by a procession of craft dressed overall and carrying local dignitaries. It was headed by the steam auxiliary yacht *Norseman*, owned by S. R. Platt, a local businessman, and carrying the canal directors. It was followed by the Wallasey ferry *Snowdrop* carrying members of Manchester City Council. *Norseman* was designed by St Clare J. Byrne and built by Laird Brothers of Birkenhead in 1890. Auxiliary power was provided by an 80hp triple-expansion engine of Laird's own manufacture. *Snowdrop* was built for the Wallasey Local Board by W. Allsup & Sons, Preston, in 1884 and was a twin-screw vessel powered by two compound engines, each rated at 56½hp. In this view the procession is passing the Barton Swing Aqueduct which replaced James Brindley's historic structure. It would be interesting to know by what right *Norseman* is flying the Stars and Stripes and Barton Aqueduct the Red Ensign! (*Manchester Ship Canal*)

(*opposite above*)
Following the official opening ceremony at Trafford Wharf on 21 May 1894, Queen Victoria and her party boarded the Admiralty Yacht *Enchantress* to travel down the canal to Mode Wheel. *Enchantress* began life as the dispatch vessel *Helicon*, built at Portsmouth in 1865. Measuring 220ft × 28ft she had a measured displacement of 1,000 tons and her paddle engines were of 1,290ihp. The hull was of wood. After a career which took in several important events in the Mediterranean and the Red Sea, *Helicon* was converted to an Admiralty Yacht in 1888 and received her new name, being the third to carry it. She was sold out of service in July 1905 and broken up in 1906 (*Manchester Ship Canal*)

(*opposite below*)
Until comparatively recent times, paddle tugs were preferred for duties which involved extreme manoeuvrability and high static pull. For this reason the Manchester Ship Canal maintained a small fleet until the early 1950s, notably for holding the sterns of large, empty ships passing down the canal. *Eccles* was built in 1905 by J. T. Eltringham & Co of South Shields, a noted builder of paddle tugs. The two return-flue boilers and independent single-cylinder side-lever engines of 30in bore × 54in stroke were supplied by the neighbouring firm of Hepple & Co; working at 40psig and equipped with condensers, the engines had a combined rating of 66hp. *Eccles* was scrapped at Barrow in Furness in 1953, but her sister *Old Trafford*, built 1907, enjoyed further service at Seaham Harbour, bearing the name *Reliant*. Through the efforts of the Paddle Steamer Preservation Society, *Reliant* was eventually preserved in the National Maritime Museum at Greenwich (*Manchester Ship Canal*)

TUG ECCLES.

Passenger Craft

It was on water rather than rail that took place one of the most significant developments in recorded history, the adoption of mechanical propulsion. This is all too readily overlooked by those who are dazzled by the success of the steam locomotive, yet steam propulsion was firmly established on inland and coastal waters a decade before the Rainhill Trials in 1829. Within a year of the first regular steam services in Europe, operated by Bell's *Comet* in 1812, steam craft were appearing in several parts of Britain. An improvised steamer began running between Norwich and Yarmouth in 1813, while on the opposite side of the country the *Charlotte* was launched for service on the River Severn, a short-lived and unsuccessful venture as it turned out. The year 1814 saw the first regular services between Hull and Gainsborough on the lower Trent, and from then on steamers appeared all over the place.

Some of these early ventures had a comic fatalism about them. In 1821 the Severn Steam Yacht Company launched their twin-hulled steam yacht (sic) *Sovereign* for a second attempt at regular services on the Severn. Something had gone wrong with their calculations, for the boat drew too much water and within a few months was up for sale 'admirably adapted for a floating bath'. It was followed by the more conventional single-hulled boat *The Twins*, which went into service just as the company itself went into liquidation. The truth is that the technology of high-pressure steam engines, like the operating practice necessary for powered craft, was new and took time to assimilate; the wonder is not that there were failures but that there were so many quick successes. Virtually all these early steamers used non-condensing high-pressure engines (anything over 15psig was considered 'high') and all were propelled by paddle wheels. Not until some years later did condensers become common, opening the way for compound engines of greatly increased efficiency. All early paddle wheels were non-feathering, an additional cause of inefficiency which made it easier for the screw propeller to gain acceptance in the 1840s. The later feathering wheel is probably the most efficient means of propelling a boat yet devised, but has limitations when applied to seagoing craft.

One can do no more than highlight a few of the inland steamer services that once operated in Britain, of which the more notable were those on certain Scottish lochs, in the English Lake District and on some of the larger English rivers like the Severn and Thames. Many of these were once year-round, scheduled services that formed an integral part of the nation's transport network, but with the spread of railways and the subsequent development of road transport their importance declined and they became purely tourist operations, often restricted to the summer months. It is in this form that two services remained steam powered in 1981, on Loch Lomond (PS *Maid of the Loch*) and Loch Katrine (SS *Sir Walter Scott*). Many others survive as services but no longer use steam, having succumbed to the persuasive sales talk of the oil industry. Long may the survivors continue in steam, but we should not forget that they will do so only if they are patronised by those who wish to ensure their survival. Even as we write, the Loch Lomond steamer has been laid up and its future is in doubt.

Services to the Highlands and Islands of Scotland involved the use of both the Crinan and Caledonian canals. Early steamers were small enough to use the canals, but eventually the regular passenger vessels were too large to do so, certainly as far as the Crinan was concerned, and so special canal steamers had to be used. The unusual twin-screw *Linnet* operated on the Crinan Canal throughout the last sixty-odd years of this service, the seaward legs of which were provided by larger and more widely celebrated members of the legendary MacBrayne fleet. David MacBrayne was synonymous with West Highland transport for many years, and among other craft to carry their colours were the two venerable paddle steamers that maintained the service between Fort William and Inverness along the Caledonian Canal. Oldest of all in the MacBrayne fleet was the *Glengarry*, formerly *Edinburgh Castle*, which was built in 1844 and operated the canal service from 1846 until she was withdrawn in 1927. Somewhat younger was the famous *Gondolier*, built 1866 and withdrawn when the service ended for good on the outbreak of war in 1939. Both these were basically seagoing paddle steamers used on inland waters, though any craft that operated Loch Ness in winter had to be thoroughly seaworthy.

Several Scottish lochs enjoyed steamer services in more leisurely days. Most northerly of all was Loch Maree, where in 1883 the steam launch *Mabel* began a service linking Rhu Nohar, the Loch Maree Hotel and Tollie. It became part of the MacBrayne empire in 1887 and remained in use until 1913. In 1894 one could do a round trip lasting three days from Oban to Gairloch for just under £3; outward by way of Skye and inward by coach to Achnasheen, train to Inverness and steamer through the Caledonian Canal, including a trip down Loch Maree. Local interests began steamer services on more inland lochs such as Katrine, Tay and Rannoch. These were operated primarily for the benefit of communities around their shores, later cashing in on tourism, and used specially built screw steamers that often carried freight and livestock as well as passengers. The *Sir Walter Scott* on Loch Katrine is a living example of this class of steamer.

Despite the intense competition it suffered from parallel railways, the Forth & Clyde Canal still boasted a passenger service of sorts as late as 1881, latterly by a private operator using the canal steamer *Rockavilla Castle*. After a break of twelve years, pleasure services again began using the first of the famous 'Queens' operated by James Aitken & Co of Kirkintilloch. They were purpose-built steamers of the largest size permitted on the canal, having three decks and full dining facilities. Unusually for their time, they were one-class vessels right from the start. Summertime cruises on the Forth & Clyde Canal were an established and popular feature of Scottish life for two generations, and there was widespread regret when the services were abandoned after the 1939 season.

Lake steamers were for many years a feature of the larger English lakes, too. Pride of place in this category must go to the unique *Gondola* on Lake Coniston, one of the most unusual steamers ever built. It was designed by James Ramsden, of the Coniston Railway, for the dukes of Devonshire and Buccleuch in 1859. As built it was virtually an enormous gondola powered by an invisible steam engine, though unlike the true gondola it was symmetrical. No funnel was fitted, exhaust being ducted to ports just above the waterline at the stern. The elegant hull was adorned with mouldings based on the family crests of her joint owners. After the Coniston Railway became part of the Furness Railway in 1862, *Gondola* was added to the FR steamer fleet and was subsequently remodelled with a conventional funnel and wheel steering. She continued to operate a regular service until 1939, but after being laid up through the war she was sold for conversion to a houseboat in 1946 and her machinery removed. (The story of *Gondola* is continued in Chapter 8.)

Windermere saw its first steamer in 1846, and a few years later there began regular services along the lake which are still running today, though not by steam. Following the completion of the Furness Railway branch to Lakeside in 1867, the FR absorbed the lake steamers in 1872 and proceeded to develop one of the most elegant fleets in the country. All their new vessels had steel hulls of particularly pleasing shape, and all but one were twin screw. Some of them retained the old arrangement found in early seagoing twin-screw vessels, the engines being laid horizontally across the hull, one in front of the other. The later vessels of this fleet are still in service with British Rail (Sealink), but were converted to diesel power in the 1950s. With the increasing cost of oil, might one perhaps hope that, say, *Tern* is restored to steam power for her centenary in 1991?

Moving south, one may mention the steamer services operated on the rivers Severn and Avon by Bathurst's of Tewkesbury. This yard was founded in 1847, and although the original company failed in the 1920s, it existed under its original name until comparatively recent times. The authors remember seeing a number of small steam launch engines dumped behind the premises in the early 1950s, victims of the craze for 'modernity'; what would those engines be worth today? Bathurst's steamers were unusual, as far as the subjects of this book are concerned, in being of wooden construction - teak planking on Canadian Rock Elm frames - their builders being of course more familiar with such construction than with metalwork. Engines were purchased from

local builders and the vessels finished in the highest traditions of Victorian craftsmanship. They built three steamers between 1887 and 1902, the newer vessels remaining in service until the 1950s and then being sold for service elsewhere. During World War I, the two larger vessels *King* and *River Queen* operated a general freight and passenger service between Sharpness and Tewkesbury, one working on the Gloucester & Berkeley Canal and the other up river from Gloucester Docks. It may be mentioned here that a passenger service survived on the Gloucester & Berkeley Canal until 1927, serving small communities that were, until the advent of motor transport, quite isolated. Three small steamers, *Kestrel, Wave* and *Lapwing*, operated this service, being built locally by Seekings & Co.

On the River Thames the Oxford & Kingston Steamboat Co tried to establish a regular service along the more popular length of the river in the mid-1880s. They failed, but the potential of such a service was recognised by Salter Bros of Oxford, possibly the most famous builder and operator of pleasure boats on the entire river. Salter took over the Oxford & Kingston fleet in 1888 but quickly replaced it with their own purpose-built steel launches, constructed to their own specification by Edwin Clarke of Brimscombe. These launches were delivered to the Thames by way of the Kennet & Avon Canal and some of them later made the return journey when sold to operators on the Severn and Warwickshire Avon. Four of these launches appeared between 1889 and 1892, being replaced by larger vessels from Salter's own yard at Iffley some twenty years later. Power for the new launches was provided by triple-expansion engines from the well-known Gloucester firm of Sissons, makers of small steam plant down to the present day. These elegant craft lasted into the 1950s and the authors can recall Sunday afternoons spent sailing from Marlow to Reading in almost total silence on one or other of them. It was perhaps the last river service to be operated in the traditional manner, belonging to an age when style was not subservient to expediency, and though the boats still ran after they had been converted to diesel power the magic was no longer there.

(*top*)

One of the more unusual craft to sail on British waters is the Lake Coniston steamer *Gondola*. Built by Jones & Quiggan of Liverpool in 1859, it was erected on the shores of the lake and remained in use for some eighty years. After a long period of disuse, it has recently been restored by the National Trust, but unfortunately the original iron hull was beyond repair and the present vessel has a new steel hull embodying certain parts of the original. Power for this unusual vessel was provided by a small locomotive boiler and inverted diagonal engine at the stern, the engine being below the boiler barrel and built into the hull structure. As built, the exhaust was taken out through the stern to avoid visible smoke or steam, but after the boat came into Furness Railway ownership in 1862 it was modified to the state in which it is seen here. The photograph was taken at Coniston boathouse in the 1890s (*Collection, A. D. Smith*)

(*above*)

The Furness Railway provided the elegant twin-screw steamer *Tern* for its Windermere services in 1891. It came from Forrest's yard at Wivenhoe, Essex, and had engines by Westray, Copeland of Barrow. This was one of the steamers with the old layout of staggered transverse engines. The unusual hull shape was repeated on other Lake District steamers. *Tern* was converted to diesel power in 1958, and is still in service, little altered in appearance apart from the fitting of a larger funnel more in keeping with a motor vessel (*G. Langmuir*)

When she was withdrawn at the end of 1927, MacBrayne's Caledonian Canal steamer *Glengarry* was not only the oldest vessel in the fleet but the oldest working steamer in the world. She was built for service on Loch Long and Holy Loch by Smith & Rodger as far back as 1844, transferring to the Caledonian Canal in 1846, and until 1875 carried the name *Edinburgh Castle*. She came into MacBrayne's ownership in 1860 and became the last vessel to carry the original colours of that company, retaining a black top to her red funnel to the end. *Glengarry* was also the last vessel in regular service with a single-cylinder steeple engine, this having been made by David Napier, cousin of the more famous Robert. The steeple engine was at one time quite popular because it was mechanically straightforward yet gave a low centre of gravity. The cylinder was directly below the paddle shaft, but the crosshead was well above the shaft and connected to the piston by multiple piston rods descending either side of the shaft itself. In this photograph *Glengarry* is seen near Fort Augustus at the northern end of the canal (*Stormier-Vogt Collection, per G. Langmuir*)

(opposite below)
For more than sixty years, passengers on MacBrayne's direct Glasgow–Oban sailings had to disembark at Ardrishaig or Crinan and transfer to the Crinan Canal steamer *Linnet* for the short trip across the isthmus. *Linnet* was built for J. & G. Thomson of Dumbarton in 1866 and featured another space-saving layout of twin-screw machinery that enjoyed brief popularity. Each shaft was driven by its own two-cylinder simple engine, but the two engines were combined into a

single A-shaped unit with four cylinders at the apex and two crankshafts at the feet of the legs. Two locomotive boilers were mounted across the hull, their fireboxes being outboard and their smokeboxes in the centre of the hull beneath the single funnel. The hull itself was of typically elegant form but completely overshadowed by the tall superstructure. After the addition of a deckhouse and funnel extension in 1894, the vessel looked even more top-heavy. The direct service operated only during the summer months, and *Linnet* was withdrawn at the end of the 1929 season. Sold to the Glasgow Motor Boat Club, she became a floating club house off Shandon in the Gare Loch and sank during a storm in January 1932 (*G. Langmuir*)

(above)
It is still possible to enjoy steam propulsion on Loch Katrine. This photograph taken at Trossachs Pier in the 1890s shows the immediate predecessor of today's *Sir Walter Scott*, the second *Rob Roy*. This vessel was built by Alexander Denny of Dumbarton in 1859 to replace an earlier one of the same name, and had an engine by T. Wingate & Co of Glasgow. This may have been an orthodox two-cylinder simple or a three-cylinder oscillating engine; Wingate supplied both types for vessels of this size at the time. The combination of clipper bow and transom stern was somewhat unusual in a lake steamer, but the lifeboat hung in davits at the stern was no ornament. Many Scottish lochs are deeper than the North Sea and can become just as dangerous in a storm. *Rob Roy* is understood to have lasted until c1911, *Sir Walter Scott* having arrived in 1900, but her ultimate fate is unknown (*Collection, C. P. Weaver*)

The Loch Tay Steamboat Co Ltd was set up by the Marquis of Breadalbane in 1882 to improve communications along the shores of the loch, most inhabitants being his tenants. A maximum of four steamers was operated by this company, carrying not only passengers but general freight and livestock. The twin-screw *Queen of the Lake* was built by the Ailsa Shipbuilding Co Ltd of Troon in 1907, transported to Killin in sections and assembled on the slipway there. Two compound engines, each of 21½nhp, gave her a speed of 13 knots. In 1922 the steamers were taken over by the Caledonian Railway, of which the original company was probably a subsidiary in all but name, Breadalbane being a director of the CR for many years and having a locomotive named after him. *Queen of the Lake* was the last survivor of the fleet, remaining at work until 1939. Laid up during World War II, she was broken up in 1950 after a survey had shown that repairs were uneconomic. She is seen here laid up on the slipway at Kenmore in 1946, from where she would never sail again. (*Collection, C. P. Weaver*)

It was appropriate that the last regular steam passenger services on a British canal should operate on the Forth & Clyde. From 1893 until 1939 the 'Queens' of James Aitken & Co provided summer-time excursion services from their base at Kirkintilloch. *Gipsy Queen* was the largest of the fleet, built to the maximum possible dimensions for a canal steamer by Bow, McLachlan & Sons Ltd of Paisley in 1905. She was powered by a single two-cylinder compound engine and had three decks. The Queens were single-class vessels from the start, and had full dining facilities. So popular were these services that Bob Smith's Ideal Band enjoyed great success in and around Glasgow during the 1930s with a composition entitled *Canal Cruise*, set on the *Faery Queen*. *Gipsy Queen* worked the last services in 1939 and was sold for scrap in 1940 (*Strathkelvin Libraries*)

The River Tay steamer *Carlyle* was one of thirty small paddle steamers built in 1904–5 for the London County Council's projected passenger service along the Thames from Hammersmith to Greenwich. An ill-conceived project, the service was a financial disaster and ceased in October 1907, most of the steamers being sold for service elsewhere in Britain and also to overseas customers. *Carlyle* was one of eleven identical vessels built for the service by the Thames Iron Works at Canning Town. Measuring 130ft × 22ft (over paddleboxes), she had a compound diagonal engine of 16in/31in bore × 36in stroke, 41nhp, and a single 'Scotch' boiler with Howden forced draught. In 1909 she was sold to the Tay Steamboat Co Ltd, Dundee, who sold her to George Martin less than two years later. Martin operated her on the Tay until 1916 when she was sold to one H. G. Kelloch, after which nothing more is heard of her. In this photograph, taken about 1914, *Carlyle* is disembarking passengers at Bridge of Earn, at a point adjacent to the main road and to the Caledonian Railway station (*Dundee Museums & Art Galleries*)

The *John Stirling* was named after the chairman of the North British Railway under whose guidance the estuaries of the Forth and Tay were bridged. She was built for the NBR's ferry service between Granton and Burntisland, the predecessor of the Forth Bridge, and launched from the Kinghorn yard of J. Key & Sons in 1876. Her two-cylinder simple oscillating engine (54in bore × 51in stroke) developed 250hp and came from Key's engineering works at Kirkaldy. Rendered surplus by the opening of the Forth Bridge in 1890, *John Stirling* was in 1892 sold to P. & W. MacLellan, who took her first to the Clyde and then to the Manchester Ship Canal. This view shows her on the latter waterway in 1894, still in MacLellan colours and operating an excursion shortly after the canal was opened. Her ultimate fate is not known (*Manchester Ship Canal*)

Steamer services on the lower Trent between Gainsborough and Hull began as early as 1814 and were for many years in the hands of the Gainsborough United Steam Packet Co Ltd. One of their vessels was the iron paddle steamer *Scarborough* of 1866. The builder is not recorded, but she had a two-cylinder simple oscillating engine by J. Penn & Sons with cylinders 30in bore × 34in stroke. This photograph shows *Scarborough* in the lower reaches of the Trent sometime early in the present century. Like most of the services on the Humber and its associated waterways, the Gainsborough–Hull one was a victim of road transport, and it is believed that *Scarborough* was scrapped during or just after World War I (*Collection, Alan Faulkner*)

Representative of the many small launches that operated regular pleasure services on our major rivers in the early years of this century is the *Alma* of Bedford, seen below Town Bridge sometime around 1906. The launches here were introduced in 1902 and taken over by the Bedford Steam Boat Co in 1911. After operating through World War I, the fleet was somewhat run down, and when electric launches were introduced in 1919 only the best of the steamers were converted. *Alma* had been laid up awaiting repair and was not converted; it is believed that her remains now lie somewhere on the bed of the river (*M. Palmer; Collection, Alan Faulkner*)

(*top*)

This superb photograph shows the graceful steamers built and operated by Bathurst's of Tewkesbury. All three are present in this view of Grove's yard at Evesham, together with the Worcester & Birmingham Canal launch *Swallow*, another Bathurst product. *King*, on the left, was launched in 1902 and was powered by a small triple-expansion engine made by T. & A. Savery & Co Ltd of Birmingham, the small 'Scotch' boiler being made by Abbott & Co of Newark. *King* worked until the 1960s and was then sold for service at Bristol, a diesel engine being fitted. *River Queen* dated from 1899 and had compound machinery by Sissons of Gloucester; she, too, was

sold to an operator in Bristol when Bathurst had finished with her. Both vessels were operated by a crew of three and among their equipment was a Windermere steam kettle of 5 gallons capacity. *Jubilee* was the oldest of the trio, dating from 1887, and had a two-cylinder simple engine (*D. W. Vickerage*)

(*above*)

Another view of Bathurst's fleet taken in 1907 shows *Jubilee* passing through the antique navigation weir at Pershore. Two of these devices survived on the Warwickshire Avon until they were removed by the Lower Avon Navigation Trust in the 1950s. *Jubilee* was sold to an operator on the Thames in 1936 and taken there by way of the semi-derelict Kennet & Avon Canal, taking two weeks to cover the fifty-seven miles between Bath and Newbury. Philip Weaver assisted the crew to get along a particularly bad section near Bradford-on-Avon on that occasion. In those days it was rare for a boat to attempt the passage through the canal and *Jubilee* was one of the last to do so before it became derelict (*D. W. Vickerage*)

(*right*)
Salter Brothers of Oxford were at one time almost synonymous with boating on the River Thames. The firm dates from 1858, and began its famous steamer service between Kingston and Oxford in 1888. The second generation of steel-hulled boats built for this run lasted under steam into the late 1950s, before succumbing to the allegedly superior economics of diesel power. *Goring* was one of the last to be converted, and is seen here at Bray Lock on 7 June 1913. She was launched from Salters' own yard at Iffley in 1912, being equipped with a 'Scotch' boiler by Abbott of Newark and a Sissons triple-expansion engine. The latter was works No 1039, having cylinders 6in/8¼in/11in × 8in and indicating 65hp (*Hertford County Records Office; Collection, Alan Faulkner*)

Typical power for the larger river steamer was a triple-expansion engine such as this superb example of Messrs Sissons' wares. Works No. 3113 powered the Salter steamer *Cliveden*, having cylinders 6in/8in/11in × 8in and working at 200psig; like the engine of *Goring*, it would develop around 65ihp. Sissons used their own radial valve gear, a derivative of Marshall gear. The latter was itself a derivative of the archetypal Hackworth gear of 1859, the first radial gear to challenge Stephenson link motion in marine applications (*W. Sisson & Co Ltd; Collection, C. P. Weaver*)

Inspection Launches

Inspection launches were used by a number of waterway managements, either for engineering inspections carried out by their staff or for more general inspections by the proprietors themselves. There was also a select band of private launches whose owners undertook lengthy tours of the waterway network and recorded what they saw. Because their accounts are first-hand records of our waterways in their heyday, they are an important contribution to transport history.

Powered inspection craft were rare until the 1870s, partly because the development of steam launches lagged behind that of larger vessels due to the need for more compact power plants and partly because of resistance to powered craft in general. The earliest inspection launch of which we have record was *Dawn*, purchased by the Severn Commissioners from Hunter & Co of Worcester in 1857. Details of her machinery are lacking, but it would not be far off the mark to assume that a small locomotive or vertical firetube boiler supplied steam to a single-cylinder inverted (vertical) engine and that no condenser was fitted. The year 1870 saw the introduction of the locally built *Sabrina* on the neighbouring Gloucester & Berkeley Canal. This vessel served its intended purpose virtually unaltered for over seventy years and is still afloat under steam, though not with her original machinery.

It was in 1870 that the Birmingham Canal Navigations bought a second-hand steam launch (builder unrecorded) that was overhauled by Yarrow's Shoreditch yard before delivery. Named *Selene* by her new owners, this craft was much used for inspection purposes until completely superseded by the motor car in the early 1930s. She did not remain steam powered for very long, however, for the BCN was a subsidiary of the London & North Western Railway and no more let the grass grow under its feet than did the 'Premier Line'. As early as 1906 the steam engine was removed from *Selene* and replaced by a petrol engine built in their own workshops at Ocker Hill, near Tipton, an early example of such conversion. At times the BCN also made use of the LNWR to visit several points on the system in a single day, the famous locomotive *Cornwall* being assigned to this duty, hauling the Chief

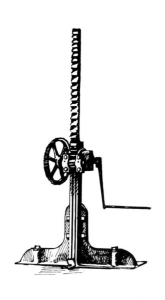

Mechanical Engineer's saloon, on more than one occasion.

The year 1877 saw the launch of a rather enigmatic vessel, the *Herald of Peace*, by John Thompson & Co of Northwich. One of the largest and most powerful steam flats on the River Weaver, it was normally used by Thompson as a commercial vessel but was in fact a dual-purpose boat fitted, latterly, with acetylene lighting and capable of conversion to a well-equipped inspection steamer. In the latter form it was often hired by the trustees of the River Weaver Navigation, despite the fact that they had more than one inspection launch of their own. Why they chose to do so is as big a mystery as the operation of a dual-purpose vessel by a private owner in the first place. The *official* inspection launch of the Weaver trustees was the *Delamere*, built by Edwin Clarke of Brimscombe in 1887. She was of narrow-boat proportions to permit operation on the adjoining Trent & Mersey Canal, but unfortunately was too high to travel far on that waterway. In 1887 she was rebuilt to a lower and less elegant profile to allow more general canal use, and in this form was used by the trustees' engineer, Col J. A. Saner, for two lengthy canal tours. The first, in 1891, was a fact-finding tour as part of his campaign for improvement of the main canal system; the second was in 1906 when he travelled to London by canal to present his ideas to the Royal Commission on Inland Waterways of that year. It might be thought that the trustees hired the *Herald of Peace* because *Delamere* was too small for their official inspections when it seemed to be standard practice to include their families, but they had two larger vessels of their own, the passenger tugs *Pioneer* and *Volunteer*, which could offer the same standard of accommodation.

Inspection launches that were also tugs were not uncommon. Since 1929 the official canal tender of the Manchester Ship Canal has been the passenger tug *Daniel Adamson* (*Ralph Brocklebank* until 1936), built to haul barges across the Mersey from Ellesmere Port to Liverpool, a service on which passengers were carried until the early 1920s. *Daniel Adamson* is still in commission and retains the original engines, the last survivor of its kind. A smaller passenger tug

was *Swift*, the official inspection launch of the Grand Junction Canal. As built in the late nineteenth century, this was an unusually ugly craft, the large fore-cabin being quite out of proportion with the rest of the boat and of totally different construction. In 1905 it was rebuilt as a proper inspection launch capable of undertaking long voyages, a living cabin being added at the stern for accommodation of the crew. A new, probably smaller, power plant was installed at this time.

No canal was more lavish with inspection launches than the Leeds & Liverpool. Within a few years of introducing steam commercial craft, it provided the committee with a steam barge (sic) of similar specification, later named *Water Witch*. In 1915 a proper launch was built to replace it, the name being perpetuated on the new boat, and this remained in use until 1951. Besides the committee launch, the Leeds & Liverpool also provided launches for its engineers and one each for its other officials based in Yorkshire and Lancashire. It must be presumed that the traditional trans-Pennine rivalry precluded the use of a single boat by both groups!

The first private explorer of the waterway network was Peter W. Willans in his launch *Black Angel*. Willans is best remembered as the inventor of the high-speed centre-valve engine that was widely used for electrical generation in the early days of that industry, but he had earlier invented a three-cylinder, totally enclosed launch engine, and it was to try out this engine that *Black Angel* was built in 1876. In the Willans launch engine there was no separate valve gear, steam distribution being by piston valves on extensions of the piston rods. Valve events being symmetrical, it was possible to reverse the engine by reversing the steam and exhaust ports, this being done by a disc valve on the side of the engine that also acted as a throttle. The engine was notable as being the first to employ splash lubrication from an enclosed sump. It ran at the surprisingly high speed for those days of 600rpm, and must have required something rather special in the way of propeller design. On 4 August 1876 Willans and a friend set out from Henley-on-Thames and by 15 August had reached the 'farthest north' of the English waterway system at Ripon by way of Brentford, the Grand Junction and Grand Union canals and the rivers Trent and Ouse. On this trip he covered the 103 miles from Newark to York in a single day, during which *Black Angel* was in steam for eighteen hours. As two and a half hours were spent aground in the lower reaches of the Trent and more time was lost at a 'difficult' lock, the actual travelling time cannot have exceeded twelve hours. For a two-man crew to maintain 8½mph over waterways carrying heavy commercial traffic was no mean achievement, and it is one unlikely to be repeated today.

Henry Rodolph de Salis was a director of Fellows, Morton & Clayton Ltd, and like his contemporary, Col Saner, deeply interested in development of the waterway system. After some preliminary explorations in hired vessels or on foot, he purchased the 33ft steam launch *Dragon Fly* in 1891 and began a series of tours that were to take him over virtually every mile of navigable waterway in England and Wales. A second, larger *Dragon Fly* was obtained in 1893 but did not satisfy his requirement for a simple, rugged boat that could be taken up the worst possible waterway. De Salis therefore designed his own boat and had it built by George Davis of Abingdon in 1895. The third *Dragon Fly* was a 59ft steel narrow boat powered by a large two-cylinder simple engine driving a special forged steel weed-slipping propeller whose blades were tangential to the boss, this being mounted between the stern and rudder posts and protected by the skeg beneath it. A locomotive boiler of generous proportions was provided for operation on bad water, the engine being non-condensing for simplicity.

De Salis began his first trip in the new boat on 17 June 1895, making a complete sweep around the northern waterways that covered

1,013 miles and included 674 locks. He did not travel as fast as Willans, being primarily concerned with making an accurate record of the canals and rivers through which he passed. The mass of statistical and technical information collected on these tours was eventually published as *Bradshaw's Canals and Navigable Rivers of England and Wales* in 1904, an all-time classic of canal literature. As his records for this purpose became more detailed, he appears to have stopped keeping a detailed log of *Dragon Fly*'s travels as a separate entity. We know that she went through Sapperton Tunnel in 1895 and negotiated the antique navigation works of the Warwickshire Avon in the summer of 1896, but the next we hear is that by 1901 she had covered 14,340 miles and passed through 5,125 locks. De Salis sold her in 1907 and she is believed to be the same *Dragon Fly* that was subsequently converted to a pump boat on the Grand Junction Canal, using the old machinery from their *Swift*. Could this have been the derelict pump boat that the authors remember lying at Hatton Wharf in the early 1950s?

The Leeds & Liverpool Canal was lavish in the provision of launches for the use of its senior officials. Those based in Lancashire could enjoy this classic example of the Victorian boatbuilder's art, appropriately named *Victoria*. It was bought second-hand for £125 in November 1898, and from what can be seen of the boiler mountings and other details must have been built at least ten years earlier (*Craven Museum; Collection, N. Walls*)

Another traveller of the same period, though for rather different reasons, was D. W. Noakes, official photographer of the Port of London Authority. Noakes was the inventor of an elaborate multiple magic lantern known as the Noakesoscope, for which he prepared a number of spectacular slide shows, including one titled *England bisected by a Steam Launch*. This was based on a series of photographs taken during a tour in the steam launch *Lizzie*, to which was added a series of animation slides. Fortunately this unique entertainment has survived both the ravages of time and the successive triumphs of the motion picture and of the cathode-ray tube.

No list of canal explorers can omit the late L. T. C. Rolt and his travels in the narrow boat *Cressy*, his account of which was published in 1944 under the title *Narrow Boat* and quickly became a classic of its kind. It is no exaggeration to claim that *Narrow Boat* was one of a handful of books in similar vein that launched the whole preservation/industrial archaeology movement in this country. It is as the youthful engineer of a steam-powered *Cressy* that Tom Rolt deserves to be included here. In 1929 he was working with Kyrle Willans, the son of Peter W. Willans, when the latter purchased *Cressy* from Peate Bros of Maesbury on the Montgomeryshire Canal. Willans decided to install a steam plant consisting of a Yorkshire steam wagon double-ended boiler and a two-cylinder compound engine by Plenty & Sons of Newbury. Rolt acted as engineer during trials of this massive but unsatisfactory installation, but Willans soon lost interest and the boat was sold. Its new owner installed a Ford Model T engine, and it was in this form that Rolt bought her some years later and commenced his historic travels.

As a tailpiece to this chapter of canal inspections, it may be recorded that the first *airborne* meeting of a board of directors took place in December 1931 when the Sheffield & South Yorkshire Navigation chartered a Westland Wessex for an aerial inspection of their waterway. Nobody could ever accuse the managements of our northern waterways of lacking initiative.

(*opposite above*)
The Yorkshire counterpart of *Victoria* was *Alexandra*, which for some reason is not mentioned in the Leeds & Liverpool minute books. It may, however, have been the *Dart* which was purchased in July 1897 for the extremely low price of £85; this too was for use in Yorkshire, and the price suggests that it was in need of a refit during which the name could have been changed. Like so many Leeds & Liverpool photographs, this was taken at the top of the Bingley Five-rise with Newton Grange in the background (*Collection, C. P. Weaver*)

(*left*)
Sabrina of the Gloucester & Berkeley Canal was one of the first powered inspection craft. She was built by Fielding & Platt of Gloucester in 1870 and was fitted with one of their standard launch power plants consisting of a small return-tube boiler on the back of which was mounted a single-cylinder engine. Very little alteration was made during her seventy-four years' service on the canal and she is seen here in August 1938 taking the then Minister of Transport, Dr Leslie Burgin, on a tour of the canal installations (*Gloucester Newspapers Ltd; Collection, Dr H. Pereira*)

Two Leeds & Liverpool boats carried the name *Water Witch*. This is the second one, built at the company's Wigan yard in 1915 to replace the original committee barge of 1878. Little has survived in the way of technical details, despite the fact that she remained in service in original form until 1951, being then sold for conversion to a motor cruiser (*Craven Museum; Collection, N. Walls*)

(*opposite above*)

This photograph is an excellent example of the way in which careful examination can reveal far more interesting detail than is at first apparent. The intended subject is a group of Grand Junction Canal directors seated in the fore-end of their inspection launch *Swift*. Among them we can pick out the bearded profile of Rodolph Fane de Salis, last chairman of the GJCC from 1914 until the amalgamation that produced the Grand Union Canal in 1929. Fane de Salis, his full surname, was only very distantly related to H. R. de Salis of *Bradshaw* fame, with whom he is sometimes confused. *Swift* was not always as neatly proportioned as we see her in this view, having been a combined tug and inspection launch with the large fore-cabin only until rebuilt in 1905. When rebuilt she received new machinery supplied by A. H. Beasley & Sons of Uxbridge. Close examination of *Swift* reveals an early Evinrude outboard motor carried on the front of the rear cabin, probably to save lighting up the steam plant when the boat had only to be moved a short distance. Tied up across the canal is a unique narrow boat, the *Mermaid*. Owned by N. Hingley & Sons Ltd of Netherton Iron Works, she was originally built for John I. Thornycroft Ltd and used as a test bed for their suction gas engine in an early challenge to the steam narrow boat. After completion of rather inconclusive trials, she was sold to Hingley, retaining the suction gas engine and wheel steering. Hingley had strong connections with yet another form of boat propulsion, for they were at this time arguably the world's leading chainmakers and supplied much of the heavy submerged chain on which operated the cable tugs of European rivers like the Neckar, Moselle and Elbe (*Waterways Museum*)

(*opposite below*)

Another Grand Junction launch was the *Gadfly*, operated by their Northern District engineer, T. W. Millner. He was responsible for everything north of Leighton Buzzard from 1896 until 1929, and we are fortunate that he was a keen photographer, recording much that happened in his territory. *Gadfly* was used for general inspections and social occasions, being too slow and inflexible for the rapid gathering of information. For this purpose Millner was an early user of a motor cycle. *Gadfly* was the first boat to pass through the Foxton inclined plane lift when it was opened on 10 July 1900. On a less formal occasion, she is posed near the east end of Braunston Tunnel carrying Millner (in cap, seated under the canopy), his family and some friends on a boating picnic (*Waterways Museum*)

(*above*)

Edwin Clarke of Brimscombe built the narrow inspection launch *Delamere* for the River Weaver in 1870. Being rather too tall for general use on the adjoining canal system, she was reconstructed in 1887 and subsequently used by Col J. A. Saner for fact-finding tours of the canal system. She is seen here in her original form. *Delamere* was sold to a Mr Caldwell of Warrington in 1938 and converted to a motor cruiser (*Waterways Museum*)

(*opposite above*)
Ouse Tender was originally owned by the Mersey Docks & Harbours Board, for whom she was built in 1883, and bought by the Aire & Calder Navigation in 1900. It served as a surveying and inspection launch on the lower part of the River Ouse for more than sixty years, normal duties being regular, sometimes daily, survey trips between Hook and Trent Falls, a stretch of river on which the deep channel is forever changing. It also worked a weekly trip to Blacktoft Jetty, weather permitting. *Ouse Tender* was steam powered until 1953 and finally withdrawn from service in 1962 (*Collection, Mike Taylor*)

(*opposite centre*)
Bathurst's of Tewkesbury built the inspection launch *Swallow* in the early part of the present century. She was the official inspection launch of the Worcester & Birmingham Canal, by then part of the Sharpness New Docks & Gloucester & Birmingham Navigation Co. *Swallow* had a two-cylinder compound engine and a small, side-fired locomotive boiler, both supplied by W. Sisson & Co of Gloucester. Occasionally hired by the BCN when their own *Selene* was out of commission, she was sold for conversion to a motor cruiser in 1922 and in this guise could still be seen on the canal in the early 1970s (*D. W. Vickerage*)

(*opposite below*)
On the Trent & Mersey Canal the North Staffordshire Railway operated the inspection launch *Dolly Varden*. The NSR built such a launch in the late 1860s, fitted with a locomotive-type boiler, which may well have carried this name. Our photograph, however, shows the boat presented in 1904 by Sir Thomas and Lady Salt in memory of the first Sir Thomas, who from 1883 until 1904 was chairman of the NSR. This boat clearly has a vertical boiler. In later years it was fitted with a longer and plainer superstructure. When photographed around 1905, she was apparently carrying a family party, as were other official launches when captured by the camera. Were official inspections too hectic, or too boring, to warrant a photograph? (*Manifold Collection*)

(*above*)
One of the earliest steamer services in Britain was that across the Mersey from Liverpool to Ellesmere Port, on which the Ellesmere Canal was operating the *Countess of Bridgewater* in 1816. A century later passengers were still carried aboard the tugs of the Shropshire Union Railways & Canal Co which towed strings of barges across the estuary. In 1903 the passenger tug *Ralph Brocklebank* was built for this service by the Tranmere Bay Development Co Ltd, being equipped with two compound condensing engines by John Jones, St George's Ironworks Ltd, Liverpool. The SUR&C tugs were bought by the Manchester Ship Canal in 1922, and in 1929 *Ralph Brocklebank* became the official canal tender. During a major refit in 1936, the name was changed to *Daniel Adamson*, after the first chairman of the MSC, and in this guise the vessel is still in commission under steam (*Manchester Ship Canal*)

(left)
Peter W. Willans is seen aboard his launch *Black Angel* at Thames Ditton shortly before the start of his long canal cruise in the summer of 1876. *Black Angel* was built by Edwardes & Symes in 1875–6 and is fitted with Willans's own design of three-cylinder, totally enclosed engine, the top of which can be seen right at the stern with its single control lever well within reach of the helmsman. The boat has a small return-tube boiler fired from the front (*J. D. Willans; Collection, C. P. Weaver*)

(opposite below)
The first *Dragon Fly* owned by Henry Rodolph de Salis was this 33ft wooden launch built by Courtney & Birkett of Southwick, near Shoreham. Completed in 1891, she was used for the first of his long-distance tours and is seen here on Tixall Wide, Staffordshire & Worcestershire Canal, during the 1892 tour. Power was supplied by a small vertical multi-tubular boiler and a two-cylinder compound condensing engine (*FMC slide; Collection, C. P. Weaver*)

(below)
Third and most famous of de Salis's launches was the 59ft steel narrow boat *Dragon Fly*, launched from the St Helens, Abingdon, yard of George Davis on 23 April 1895. It was designed by de Salis himself and specifically intended to operate over shallow, dirty or weed-choked waterways. A large locomotive boiler supplied steam to a two-cylinder simple, non-condensing engine of 6¼in bore × 8in stroke, the accent being on reliability rather than efficiency. This engine drove a special weed-slipping propeller, probably of his own design, in which the blades were tangential instead of radial (*FMC slide; Collection, C. P. Weaver*)

(*opposite above*)
There is a difference between a *railway* locomotive boiler and the *marine* locomotive boiler. The former has to generate a lot of steam in a small space, whereas the latter, although a fast steamer by marine standards, must of necessity maintain its performance for hours if not days on end with the utmost reliability and a reasonably consistent efficiency. A marine boiler is therefore larger than a railway boiler of similar power, as shown by the photograph of *Dragon Fly*'s boiler. Although developing less than 50hp, it has a large firebox with a grate area of 8sq ft and 124 short firetubes (*FMC slide; Collection, C. P. Weaver*)

(*opposite below*)
Typical of the machinery that powered the smaller launches is the engine of *Little Sabrina*, another Worcester & Birmingham Canal launch. This was designed by their engineer W. F. Holborough in the early 1890s and built by George Farrin of Stoke Prior. It is a two-cylinder simple engine fitted with Stephenson's valve gear and erected on columns in the manner of a contemporary marine engine. *Little Sabrina* had an unusually short career, being withdrawn in 1918. Her engine was stored at Tardebigge Maintenance Depot, where it came to light some forty years later and was duly exhibited at Stoke Bruerne (*C. R. Weaver*)

(*above right*)
The inverted diagonal engine was popular throughout the north of England and this fine example powered the steam flat *Herald of Peace* on the River Weaver. It was made by Watt Bros of Liverpool in 1877 and with two simple-expansion cylinders (10in bore × 14in stroke) was rated at 27hp, making *Herald of Peace* one of the most powerful vessels on the river. Note the gas lighting in the engine-room, almost certainly using acetylene, and the high polish on the cylinder cleading, both explained by the boat's occasional use as an inspection launch (*Waterways Museum*)

A famous canal traveller in the engine-room of a famous boat – the late Tom Rolt and *Cressy*. Ten years before he toured the narrow canals in *Cressy*, gathering the material that would form the basis for the classic book *Narrow Boat*, Rolt was engineer on *Cressy* during her brief career as a steamboat in the ownership of Kyrle W. Willans, the son of P. W. Willans. He fitted a large double-ended Yorkshire steam wagon boiler and a Plenty two-cylinder compound, reliable enough components but too large for satisfactory operation in a narrow boat. When Rolt later bought *Cressy*, a Model T Ford petrol engine had been fitted (*Collection, C. P. Weaver*)

Maintenance Craft

Boats carrying small steam engines were in use for constructional or maintenance purposes a decade before the first successful use of steam-propelled vessels themselves. The first such vessels were pump boats used to de-water short sections of canal that could not be drained conveniently by gravity. The first recorded application was in 1794 when the famous firm of Boulton & Watt supplied a 2.8hp 'boat engine' to the Gloucester & Berkeley Canal. Herein lies a trap for the unwary historian. By 'boat engine' they meant a small, self-contained side-lever engine driving a short-stroke reciprocating pump, a unit small enough to be carried in a boat. Any thoughts that anyone might have had about adapting such an engine to propel the boat would have been dashed by James Watt, who for some reason was totally opposed to steam traction and would never allow one of his patent engines to be used for such a purpose. Steam for this tiny engine would have been supplied by a small haystack or wagon boiler, again mounted on its own framing so as to be semi-portable. The Gloucester & Berkeley pump had a steam cylinder of 23in bore × 24in stroke and was of course a Watt engine using steam at atmospheric pressure in conjunction with a condenser – high-pressure steam being another of Watt's aversions.

A number of similar pump boats were built in the next few years, notably for the Birmingham Canal, which had one in 1795 and another the following year, the Worcester & Birmingham Canal and repeat orders from the Gloucester & Berkeley. Having reciprocating bucket pumps, they were limited in pumping ability, being able only to draw from a maximum of 15–20ft below the pump and to deliver no higher than was necessary to discharge over the side of the boat, performance that was admittedly enough for many applications. The development of centrifugal pumps eventually rendered this type of pump boat obsolete, although portable suction pumps driven by small internal-combustion engines are still used for small jobs. A small number of pump boats were built with centrifugal pumps, but more often one found a boat fitted up to carry a portable engine and pump, these being used in the boat or set up on the bank as appropriate.

Next to appear was the steam dredger. Dredgers used on canals and rivers could be split into three classes: spoon dredgers, in which a large, long-handled scoop was used over the side of the boat, most of the weight being taken by a small crane while other members of the team manoeuvred the scoop using the handle; bucket ladder dredgers, in which an endless chain of buckets lifted material from the bed of the channel and discharged it into mud boats tied alongside; and grab dredgers, in which a clam-shell grab was used in conjunction with an ordinary crane. Each had its own particular advantages when applied to canal and river work. The first steam dredger on record was a spoon dredger built in 1796 for Sunderland Harbour, which is outside the scope of this book, as is the first steam-powered ladder dredger made six years later for Portsmouth Harbour. First on a canal or river was an ill-fated machine ordered by Thomas Telford for use on Loch Oich during construction of the Caledonian Canal. It was designed by his colleague William Jessop and built by the Butterley Company, in which Jessop was a partner. Erected on the shores of the loch, it was launched in October 1806 only to sink in 25ft of water through failure of a badly caulked seam. No attempt was made to recover it. This was probably the first powered dredger to incorporate the necessary feature of a friction drive to prevent damage should the buckets encounter something solid like a submerged rock.

A second dredger was built for the Caledonian Canal in 1814, beginning work in Loch Dochfour in November of that year. Used in conjunction with six specially designed mud boats, it was capable of lifting 400 tons per day. The unyielding boulder clay took its toll, however, and by 1818 it had to be rebuilt, this time using machinery supplied by Bryan Donkin. Donkin had earlier built a third dredger for the project, which began work in 1816 and carried out the tasks for which the unlucky 1806 one had been designed. This dredger was used for many years after completion of the canal and later carried the name *Glengarry*. Like some of its contemporaries it had two bucket ladders, one on either side. It was found that the single ladder working through a well in the centre of the boat was more practical and

modern dredgers are of this type.

Though widely used in rivers and harbours, ladder dredgers are of limited use in the average British canal. Canal dredging involves the removal of a thin layer of mud, often in confined spaces, whereas a river bed accumulates a considerable depth of fine and very fluid silt that has sufficient self-levelling ability to permit dredging from a few fixed positions. For these reasons the outwardly slower but far more flexible grab dredger is normally preferred for canal work. Most notable of the few bucket dredgers that have been used on our canals was the self-propelled narrow dredger *Empress*, used during the final attempt at restoration of the Thames & Severn Canal in the early years of this century. *Empress* was purchased in 1902 when she was working on the Somerset Avon near Bath, her origin being unknown. Instead of taking the direct route to her new home, up the Severn, or even going round through the Thames, she was taken there by way of Oxford and Birmingham, allegedly because repairs had to be carried out in the latter place. The last that is heard of this dredger is in 1914, when work stopped on the Thames & Severn.

The grab dredger was developed to supersede the spoon dredger, for long the only type that could work in really tight corners. The first successful grab was that developed and patented by Priestman Bros Ltd of Hull in 1877. It was a clam-shell grab operated by the main hoisting chain, dropped into the water wide open and closing as the chain was wound in to lift it. A powerful grab, it had one drawback for canal work. Because it had to be dropped on to the bottom of the canal before it could be closed, there was always a danger of bringing up the lining of puddled clay with which many canals are rendered watertight. The results of such a mistake could be catastrophic.

The answer to controlled dredging of a puddled canal was the Grafton steam grab, developed in 1894. Grafton & Co of Bedford was one of our more progressive crane manufacturers and approached the subject in characteristic fashion. The grab itself is of the usual clam-shell pattern, but is operated by a vertical steam cylinder mounted directly above it. This cylinder is carried on the end of a rigid boom mounted on the same pivots

The oldest working steam vessel in the world is the former Bridgwater Docks dredger of 1844, now preserved at the Exeter Maritime Museum after a working life of some 120 years. I. K. Brunel laid out the docks in 1841 and based their cleansing arrangements on those already in use in Cumberland Basin, Bristol, where a scraper boat dragged mud down to special sluices so that it could be flushed downriver. The Bridgwater boat is a small version of his Bristol scraper boat BD6 and was almost certainly built by Bush & Beddoes of Bristol. The large single-cylinder engine and associated machinery were made by George E. Lunell of Bristol, and apart from the boiler (replaced by the GWR) remains intact today. In this photograph the boat has winched itself to the far end of the basin on a light chain and the crew are preparing to lower the scraper blade for the next pull back to the sluices (*Douglas Allen Photography*)

as the jib of the crane, the latter being used to raise and lower the boom. The grab can therefore be lowered to a controlled depth when working over clay puddle, and it is much more powerful than a Priestman grab. The first Grafton dredger was supplied to the Grand Junction Canal in 1894, mounted on a 14ft-wide pontoon for stability. Later dredgers were carried on 7ft pontoons so that they could pass through narrow canals, additional pontoons 3ft 6in wide being attached rigidly to either side when working. A Grafton dredger can work very rapidly indeed, and although the standard steam-crane machinery was used the additional demands made by the steam ram made it necessary to provide a much larger boiler. Instead of the vertical boiler on the crane itself, therefore, a large locomotive boiler was installed at the opposite end of the pontoon and fed steam to the engines through flexible joints in the crane centre. The last Grafton dredger in regular use was built for the Grand Union Canal in 1934 and, at the time of writing, was engaged on restoration of the Basingstoke Canal.

More unusual maintenance craft were represented by one or two examples only. Pride of place among them must go to the scraper boats designed by Isambard Kingdom Brunel for Bristol and Bridgwater docks. Both docks are situated at the mouths of rivers discharging into the Severn estuary, which has the second largest tidal range in the world. This suggested that accumulated mud and silt could be disposed of by flushing it downriver on a spring tide, in which case it was merely necessary to scrape sediment across the bottom of the dock to the vicinity of the special sluices provided for its disposal. To do this Brunel devised a small boat which pulled itself backwards and forwards on long chains, dragging a scraper behind it in one direction. Use of a chain enabled a small engine to develop a very high tractive effort to overcome the resistance of the scraper, which would be difficult to achieve by the use of more conventional propulsion. So successful was this method of dredging that it survived, using the original boats, for more than a century and a quarter. The Bridgwater dredger has been preserved and is now the oldest working steamboat in the world.

Equally troublesome as mud on many Fenland waterways is water-weed. To maintain a navigation channel, it is necessary to cut this weed at regular intervals, and for this operation at least one special weed-cutter was built. Screw propellers being particularly susceptible to entanglement in floating weeds, it was propelled by special paddle wheels fitted with cutting blades. Regular trips along the waterway cut the weeds growing out from either side, thus preserving a channel of maximum width.

Our final examples of ingenious maintenance craft belonged to the Birmingham Canal Navigations. The first was the scoop-wheel pump boat built in 1894–5 for the rapid de-watering of short lengths of canal that did not possess any other means of drainage. A scoop-wheel is basically an undershot water-wheel driven backwards, lifting a large volume of water over a small difference in height, and was once used quite extensively for fen drainage. Two of the BCN pumping stations had scoop wheels, and it may have been this experience that prompted construction of their unique pump boat. The boat was in two parts. The larger piece was the 'engine boat' carrying a large boiler and the engine. It worked in conjunction with a small 'fan boat' containing the scoop-wheel, which was driven by demountable cardan shafts from the engine boat. In use the two boats were tied up on either side of the temporary dam that blocked off the affected section of canal, the fan boat being on the 'dry' side. Once in place, the latter

was sunk on to the bottom of the canal and a set of doors in one end of it were opened. The wheel was then started up, lifting water out of the canal and discharging it on to the opposite side of the temporary dam. It was a very effective pump, and even found employment as a semi-permanent recirculating pump during the erection of a new pumping station at Walsall in 1899. Without the recirculating capacity of the Walsall plant, operation of Walsall locks put an undue strain on the reservoirs supplying the Wyreley & Essington Canal. The scoop-wheel boat was therefore stationed at Dean's Bridge, on the outskirts of Wolverhampton, and during the day pumped water into the W&E. At night the process was reversed to make good the drain on the reservoirs supplying the BCN main line. Despite its efficiency, regular use of the scoop-wheel boat declined after 1906, probably because of the time taken to set it up and the growing

In this view the Bridgwater dredger is hauling itself towards the sluices on the heavier of its two haulage chains. The scraper blade is lowered on to the bottom of the basin and the engine will be working quite hard to overcome its resistance. Note that the cranes on the quayside were still steam powered when this photograph was taken in the early 1960s (*Douglas Allen Photography*)

availability of portable centrifugal pumps of equivalent capacity.

As noted earlier, the BCN was an offshoot of the LNWR and it was no coincidence that the BCN's works at Ocker Hill was the canal equivalent of Crewe. During the severe winter of 1895, traffic on the BCN came to a complete stop and the ever-inventive F. W. Webb took a hand. He sent down to Ocker Hill a number of old locomotive boilers together with sets of centrifugal pumps. Pairs of boilers were mounted in a boat together with a circulating pump. One boiler was steamed to drive the pump, the other was merely a large water heater. In operation these boats kept warm water circulating at critical points like the head of a flight of locks, thus preventing blockage by ice. The experiment had only limited success because it was impossible to stop the whole canal from freezing. Regrettably, no photograph of this interesting operation has come to light.

Ladder dredgers were rare on British canals and *Empress* was probably unique in being a self-propelled narrow canal dredger of this type. Purchased by the Thames & Severn Canal in 1902 during the last attempt at restoring that waterway, *Empress* is seen at work below Stroud Water-works at Chalford not long after arrival. The cabin was added so that her crew could live on board during operations on the rather isolated summit level of the canal. *Empress* was sold when the restoration project collapsed in 1914 (*H. G. W. Household*)

(opposite above)
Still in commission at the time of writing is the steam dredger *De Klop No 4* of the Gloucester & Berkeley Canal. Built by de Klop of Sliedrecht, Holland, in 1924, this is one of a pair, coal-fired until 1964 but now using oil. It is powered by a two-cylinder engine mounted amidships which drives both the bucket ladder and the manoeuvring winches through a friction drive. A crew of four is needed to work the dredger, which discharges overside into special mud-hopper barges. It is seen being towed out of Sharpness Docks in 1927, approaching the Severn Bridge of the former Severn & Wye Joint Railway. This was opened in October 1879 and closed after two spans were demolished on the night of 25 October 1960 following a collision between two tankers outside Sharpness Docks. The remainder of the bridge was demolished some years later (*Collection, C. P. Weaver*)

(opposite below)
The floating crane/grab dredger *Iron Duchess* was another Gloucester & Berkeley vessel. Built by Stothert & Pitt of Bath in 1943, she was used to dredge parts that could not be reached by one of the ladder dredgers. Now converted to diesel power, she is today used on the River Severn. When this photograph was taken on a dismal July afternoon in 1959, a complete dredging outfit was heading towards Sharpness behind the steam tug *Primrose* past the Timber Pool at Gloucester. *Primrose* was built at Appledore in 1908 and by 1959 was assigned to maintenance work; a few months after the authors saw her she was converted to diesel power. Also shown is one of the special 150–180 ton mud-hoppers allocated to dredging duties (*C. P. Weaver*)

(*opposite above*)
The ice-breaker/dredger *Clydeforth* was built for the Forth & Clyde Canal by D. Kyd & Co Ltd of Grangemouth in 1926. It was basically a steel Inside Puffer with rounded bows so that it could ride up on to the ice and break it by deadweight, a steam crane with dredging grab being mounted amidships. It was photographed in August 1959 passing through Garscadden Lock, Drumchapel. The following year, *Clydeforth* was converted to diesel power and transferred to the Crinan Canal, closure of the Forth & Clyde being imminent (*G. Langmuir*)

(*opposite below*)
The Grafton steam grab dredger was specifically designed for dredging to a controlled depth in a puddled canal. The first of these dredgers was supplied to the Grand Junction Canal in 1894; unlike its successors, it was mounted on a single 14ft-wide pontoon which precluded its use on narrow canals. Grafton grabs were also fitted to a number of ordinary steam cranes used to unload mud boats at landfill sites, one of which is seen in the background of this photograph taken at Braunston No 3 Mud Tip in 1910 (*Waterways Museum*)

(*above right*)
The last working Grafton dredger at the time of writing is owned by the Surrey & Hants Canal Society, and used by them on the restoration of the Basingstoke Canal. It was photographed at Dogmersfield, near Odiham, on the occasion of a visit by the Warwickshire Steam Engine Society in May 1981. This is a narrow canal dredger mounted on a 7ft pontoon, additional pontoons being attached to provide the necessary stability when actually working. It was built for the Grand Union Canal in 1934, last used by British Waterways on the Oxford Canal in 1966 and presented to the Kennet & Avon Canal Trust in 1967. The Surrey & Hants Canal Society acquired it in 1973, and after repairs at Reading it was taken to Odiham by road in July 1974. For use on the wide Basingstoke Canal, the jib and boom have been extended by 5ft (*C. R. Weaver*)

(*right*)
This close-up of the grab cylinder was taken at the moment of closing the jaws, steam being exhausted from the bottom of the cylinder. Admission of steam to the appropriate end of the cylinder is controlled by a valve on the end of the boom operated by a rod on the side nearer the camera (*C. R. Weaver*)

(*opposite above*)
Weeds can be as troublesome as mud on some waterways, notably on the Fenland network. To keep them open, the Great Ouse River Board operated the weed-cutter/pump boat *Vexem*. It was of minimal draught and propelled by special paddle wheels fitted with cutters. Power was supplied by a locomotive boiler and a large single-cylinder horizontal engine. A centrifugal pump was mounted in the stern and driven by belt from the engine flywheel, the wheel-house being dismantled when necessary to couple up the pump (*Collection, Alan Faulkner*)

(*opposite centre*)
Another cleansing duty that had to be performed in the days of steam propulsion was the removal of soot from the roof and walls of tunnels through which a tug service operated. Worst affected were Braunston and Blisworth on the Grand Junction Canal, for the sweeping of which this special brush boat was constructed. Three profiled wire brushes were kept in contact with the brickwork by pressing down on the ends of the long beams attached to the brushes. Soot thus dislodged fell into a hopper in the boat itself; no less than 10 tons was collected on its first trip through Blisworth Tunnel. Other tunnels must have faced the same problem but it is not known whether any other brush boats were used (*Waterways Museum*)

(*opposite below*)
The ice-breaker *Conway* spent its entire working life on the Crinan Canal, based at Ardrishaig. It was built by Napier, Shanks & Bell of Yoker in 1892 and provided with rounded bows so that it rode up on to ice rather than breaking it by direct impact. In summer it was used as a relief to the *Linnet*, passengers being accommodated on seats fitted to the fore-deck. When photographed at Ardrishaig in 1950, *Conway* was still in original condition with an open bridge. In 1951 it received a new boiler but was withdrawn nine years later when the dieselised *Clydeforth* became available from the Forth & Clyde Canal. Note the vintage diver's launch at the stern of the vessel (*Rev Wm Galbraith; per G. Langmuir*)

(*above*)
Canal tugs were frequently called upon to tow specialised maintenance craft such as the gate-lifting barge *GL III* on the Caledonian Canal. The original Caledonian Canal tug *Scot* is here taking *GL III* through Muirtown Locks on the outskirts of Inverness in the early 1920s. The lifting barge was converted from a World War I boom defence dumb vessel and is carrying a pair of steel-framed, oak-planked gates of the type standardised in the early twentieth century. Made in the canal workshops at Clachnaharry, each gate weighs 25 tons. Note the original capstans used to operate the lock gates, part of Telford's original design. They remained in use until the canal was mechanised in the 1960s (*British Waterways Board*)

(*opposite above*)
The steam barge *Jubilee* was built for the River Severn Commissioners by Charles Hill & Sons of Bristol in 1935. When steam powered it had a Sissons two-cylinder compound engine and single screw. A dual-purpose vessel capable of undertaking light towing duties, it was used on a range of maintenance duties and in this photograph is towing a maintenance houseboat through the narrow East Channel, about three-quarters of a mile below the Upper Parting at Gloucester. After nationalisation, it was transferred to the Gloucester & Berkeley Canal for similar duties and in 1955 converted to twin-screw diesel propulsion (*Charles Hill, Bristol Ltd*)

(*opposite below*)
One of the more unusual maintenance craft was the Birmingham Canal Navigation's scoop-wheel boat, made at their Ocker Hill works in 1894–5. In this photograph it is being used at Cappers Bridge on the Wyreley & Essington Canal not far from Huddlesford Junction, sometime around 1900. On the far side of the temporary dam, or *stank* is the *engine boat*, carrying the engine and boiler. The *fan boat* is sunk in the section of canal to be

drained and driven by a cardan shaft from the engine boat. It lifts water over the stank, the scoop-wheel being a very effective way of lifting a lot of water over a low obstacle (*David McDougall, Black Country Museum*)

(*above*)
This photograph serves to remind us that the steam engine had many other applications to waterways beside those covered in this book. The date is August 1934, a period of extreme water shortage throughout the Midland canal system. To supplement the reservoirs feeding the summit level of the Grand Union Canal, Foxton locks were closed and water pumped from the former Union Canal at the bottom of the locks, a section much better off for water. Two portable steam engines were set up on the towpath, each driving a large centrifugal pump. The engine at the bottom lifted water round the lower staircase to the pump driven by the other engine at the half-way point. Portable engines and pumps like this were sometimes used in a narrow boat when it was not convenient to set them up on the bank (*Waterways Museum*)

Archaeology and Preservation

The archaeology of the steamboat has many facets. It may indeed involve the excavation of remains in the classical manner, but it may equally consist of the study and recording of contemporary documents or photographs to build up an accurate picture of long-vanished craft, their operators and their activities. Under this heading we would place the compilation of the present book. One can but regret that so much of our industrial history has vanished without a proper record being kept. All too often we ignore history altogether or concentrate on unusual and spectacular aspects to the exclusion of everyday happenings without which there would be no history.

Perhaps the most exciting aspects of steamboat archaeology are the various projects to recover and restore to working order boats that have lain under water for many decades and have thereby survived changes in fashion, wartime scrap drives and other threats to their existence. In a modest way such recoveries have been carried out at intervals over the past forty years, but we would like to highlight two. The first, and more interesting from an historical standpoint, is the recovery of the steam launch *Dolly* from Ullswater in 1962. This elegant 40ft boat dates from the late 1850s and sank during the severe winter of 1895. She lay upright and intact until she was discovered by a sub-aqua team in 1960. Two years later she was raised using flotation bags (actually oil drums) and turned over to G. H. Pattinson for restoration. Mr Pattinson already possessed a small fleet of steam launches on Windermere, some of which he had raised from the bed of the lake. *Dolly* was taken by road over Kirkstone Pass to Windermere, towed down the lake by one of his launches and then taken out of the water for restoration to begin in earnest. The wooden hull was like blotting paper after more than sixty-five years' immersion, but by careful drying and regular application of preservative it was eventually restored to its original condition. Engine, boiler and cabin furnishings required comparatively little attention before they could be refitted to the hull, and by the middle of 1965 *Dolly* was once more afloat under steam. With other boats in the Pattinson collection she is now at the Windermere Steamboat Museum.

Much more ambitious is the current project to restore the lake steamer *Gitana* on Loch Rannoch. *Gitana* was built by T. B. Seath of Rutherglen in 1881, taken to Loch Rannoch in sections and assembled on the side of the loch. She was launched in June 1881 but operated for one season only; in January 1882 she sank in 105ft of water during a storm. Inspection by Diver Fox (who had worked on the wreckage of the Tay Bridge two years earlier) showed that recovery was impractical with the equipment then available and *Gitana* lay undisturbed on the bed of the loch for ninety-seven years. After much planning, she was raised in 1980 by a team of Scottish sub-aqua enthusiasts using flotation equipment generously donated by various manufacturers. Considering the remoteness of the site this was a notable feat, for *Gitana* is not all that much smaller than the *Mary Rose*, lifted from the sea off Portsmouth during 1982 after a much larger and more widely publicised operation. Now beached for repair, *Gitana* will require major repairs to her hull and it is proposed to construct an overlay hull of modern materials rather than attempt to repair the badly corroded platework. Engine and boiler have been removed for repair, being in fair condition. Hopefully *Gitana*, too, will one day sail again under steam.

Excavation of remains can also be an important source of historical material, sometimes bringing alive things that have long been known only on the printed page. The recent recovery of the propeller and stern-gear of the Fellows, Morton & Clayton steamer *Earl* is a good example. *Earl* was sold off to Charlie Court, an ex-FMC steam-boat captain with a reputation for damaging boats and boilers more frequently than most, and operated by him until 1937 when she sank at Stretton Stop on the Oxford Canal. The boat was by then beyond economic repair, so the engine and boiler were removed and the hull dumped in the old Brinklow Arm where *Earl*'s skeleton was to become an object of pilgrimage for a later generation of canal enthusiast. Few realised that the propeller, etc, had been left in place, but these were ultimately recovered and taken to the Waterways Museum at Stoke Bruerne. They are the only known survivals of original FMC steamer machinery, and

illustrate vividly one of the problems that beset the steamers in their early days. The FMC repair books tell us that the earlier boats had three bearings on the propeller shaft, one being behind the propeller itself. After numerous broken shafts it was realised that the outboard bearing was to blame, so the shaft extensions were cut off. Not only does the stern post of *Earl* have the housing for this outboard bearing, but the propeller shaft shows where the extension was cut off. The propeller itself is typical of those used on steamers, having a much coarser pitch than that for a comparable motor boat.

More recently there has come to light the remains of what may be an original Grand Junction Canal steamer, lying in the old brickworks basin at Up Nately on the Basingstoke Canal. The existence of this boat was not unknown, for during the last war someone removed the boiler for scrap and started to break up the engine. The top of the engine was left lying in the bottom of the boat when they gave up. It was only recently, however, that a proper examination was made, when it was realised that the boat had been fitted with a large vertical boiler and a massive single-cylinder engine of about 10hp. These features are so similar to the known specification of the Grand Junction boats as to suggest that it is one of them. If this is so, it is one of the most important discoveries yet made. As much as possible of the boat will be recovered with a view to setting up a partial reconstruction. Documentary research suggests that the boat may have been there since 1901, when traffic to the brickworks ceased, while local sources also suggest that it was dumped there after the 'Great Sale' of the Basingstoke Canal and its effects in 1904. Either way, it would appear to have been an old boat even then, which adds weight to the theory that it came from the Grand Junction fleet. By the time these words appear in print we hope to know a lot more about it.

The dividing line between archaeology and preservation is a narrow one, and we incline to the view that the only difference is in the amount of work that has to be done in acquiring the boat in the first place. Some craft that survive today have never gone out of use, a good example being the former Gloucester & Berkeley Canal inspection launch *Sabrina*. She was sold out of service and suffered the usual fate of being converted to a motor cruiser. In this form she remained active until purchased some years ago by Drs Scott and Hilary Pereira of Twickenham, who undertook restoration to something like original condition. Structurally, little had been altered but the engine and boiler had long been scrapped and there was no prospect of obtaining anything resembling the unusual Fielding & Platt design. A more modern boiler has therefore been installed together with a modern instructional steam engine.

Other craft have survived despite a lengthy period of disuse, notably the *Gondola* on Coniston. Though supposedly converted to a houseboat, this historic craft was by the early 1960s a rather pathetic sight, half-submerged and gradually rotting away. Because of her size a recovery operation such as that carried out on *Dolly* was impractical. Eventually she was taken in hand by the National Trust. A survey showed that the original hull was beyond repair, so it was cut into sections and removed to Vickers' yard at Barrow where a new steel hull was built. Locomotion Enterprises contributed a power plant of similar design to the original, modified in certain respects to meet present-day safety regulations. Eventually a new craft, containing as much as possible of the original, set sail on Coniston to continue the great traditions of Lakeland passenger

steamers. One may argue that building a new boat is not really preservation, but what is one trying to preserve? Surely a working boat that demonstrates how a commercial steamer operated and what it was like to travel or work upon one is more valuable than a heap of rusty ironwork in a museum?

Lastly, we come to a restoration project with which the authors of this book have been closely concerned. The creation of a working steam narrow boat as operated by Fellows, Morton & Clayton has long been the dream of many canal enthusiasts. One cannot say that any such boat would be a true FMC steamer, for none of the original engines and boilers have survived, nor is it possible to obtain replacements of the same design and age. It is generally the machinery that makes a steamboat interesting, except in notable cases like Brunel's *Great Britain* where the hull itself was a major advance in structural design. As noted above, this does not invalidate a reconstruction in which the character and design practices of the original

The 90ft steamer *Gitana* was launched on Loch Rannoch in 1881 and sank only seven months later. Ninety-seven years afterwards she was brought to the surface and beached near Loch Rannoch Hotel preparatory to restoration. When photographed in May 1981, she showed little sign of having spent so long under water, until one took a closer look. Then it could be seen that the iron hull was badly corroded. Current proposals are to construct a modern ferro-concrete hull around the existing structure, a technique that will produce a strong and durable structure with only an inch or so of additional material outside the iron plates, thus preserving the original lines. Engine and boiler have been removed to Perth Technical College for restoration to working order, and it is hoped one day to see *Gitana* performing again the service for which she was intended (*C. P. Weaver*)

are maintained wherever possible. The subject of this particular restoration was the former FMC steamer *President*.

Long converted to a motor boat, *President* was found some years ago by Malcolm Braine and Nicholas Bostock in a dilapidated condition sunk in the River Weaver. They decided to restore it to something like its original condition, a task which has now been successfully accomplished after extensive reconstruction of the hull and the building of a completely new superstructure. A special propeller was made, the existing one being of too fine a pitch. Restored externally in correct FMC colours and occasionally towing a restored FMC butty, *President* has attended a number of rallies since completion. Though very enjoyable, this activity has served to highlight the drawbacks of commercial steam craft on narrow canals. True, the canals were in much better condition in the days of commercial traffic than they are today, but even allowing for this the boat

makes heavy weather of things in terms of fuel consumption and maintenance. Matters are always worse when the boat is worked light for a few days only each year by a relatively inexperienced crew, but even so it is obvious that Fellows, Morton must have worked their boats (and their crews) very hard to see a reasonable return on their investment. This is no new discovery: transport economics have always been a question of size and manning levels.

That there is still scope for interesting, even surprising discoveries is demonstrated by the pieces of news that have come to us during final compilation of this book. First we learnt of the survival of the Leeds & Liverpool's *Alexandra* – hull and power plant – and of her proposed restoration. Close on the heels of that news came word that pieces of the steam barge *Nancy* had been uncovered during excavations for a new marina at Ely and finally that a change of ownership will see *President* berthed at the Black Country Museum, Dudley.

In October 1955, a chance remark led the authors to Mountsorrel on the River Soar and to the remains of the Mountsorrel Granite Co's steamer *Handy*. This was one of the last steam narrow boats, converted from a horse boat in 1928 and outwardly similar to the Fellows, Morton steamers. The power plant was second-hand, having come from a National steam bus made by Thomas Clarkson of Chelmsford. The boiler, shown in this photograph, had a central water drum and coiled water-tubes, being heated by an oil burner. The engine, which had been removed for display in the company's offices, would have been a two-cylinder simple of 4in bore × 4in stroke. Research showed that in fact *Handy* had been coal-fired, and this doubtless explained why the boiler failed on her first trip. Towed home in disgrace, the boat was abandoned and gradually disappeared from view; before any steps could be taken to salvage the boiler and stern-gear, the site was filled in and built over. Extensive enquiries failed to trace the engine which had long since disappeared from the nearby offices (*C. P. Weaver*)

(*left*)
For many years the skeleton of Fellows, Morton's *Earl* lay in a backwater of the Oxford Canal at Brinklow, undisturbed since the boat was abandoned there in February 1937 after sinking at nearby Stretton Stop. *Earl* was a wooden boat, built at Saltley in June 1895; unlike the more modern composite steamers, it was never converted to a motor boat but instead sold to the former FMC captain Charlie Court, in whose hands it saw another ten years or so of service. Despite Charlie's notoriety as a wrecker of boilers

and hulls, he kept *Earl* running long after any other steam narrow boat and was the last to trade under steam on a narrow canal (*C. P. Weaver*)

(opposite below)
In 1980 the propeller and stern-gear of *Earl* were salvaged and taken to the Waterways Museum at Stoke Bruerne. This photograph shows the remains loosely reassembled in their correct relationship. Behind the propeller is the stern post of the hull; nearer the camera is the rudder post, on the left-hand end of which is the underplate of the counter. The photograph is interesting for two reasons. Firstly, it shows that the steamers had a fixed rudder post behind the screw, unlike later motor boats in which the rudder pivoted directly in the skeg projecting rearwards from the keelson. Secondly, it shows where the third, outboard bearing for the propeller shaft was mounted in the rudder post. These bearings were a constant source of trouble, leading to shaft breakages, and were ultimately taken out, the shaft extension being cut off. *Earl*'s propeller shaft shows clearly that the end has been cut off at some time. The large cast-iron propeller is 34in diameter and has a pitch of 38in (*C. R. Weaver*)

(above)
Rescued from the remains of an old steam narrow boat that lies in the old brickworks arm at Up Nately on the Basingstoke Canal, this cylinder set in motion a salvage operation to recover what remains of a craft that almost certainly began its career with the Grand Junction Canal's carrying department in the 1860s. Regrettably, the boat attracted the attention of wartime scrap merchants who removed the boiler and started to break up the engine with the results seen here. The bottom part of the engine, together with the pumps, boiler baseplate and, almost certainly, the propeller shaft and propeller, still lie beneath the waters of the old arm. External measurements suggest that the engine has a bore and stroke of 7in × 12in and that the boiler was a vertical one of about 4ft 6in diameter. These dimensions tally with known details of the Grand Junction boats, and as this one is said to have been abandoned around 1904 this must be strong evidence that it is one of the old GJC craft. The recording and recovery of this machinery is of considerable importance as it will be one of the earliest complete examples of screw machinery to have survived (*Robin Higgs*)

One of the last Fellows, Morton steamers was *President*, built at Saltley in June 1909. Converted to a motor boat in 1925 it was last used as a maintenance boat on the River Weaver before being advertised for sale in 1973. When first seen by its new owners, Malcolm Braine and Nicholas Bostock, it was a waterlogged hulk, but after considerable effort and expenditure it has been restored to the condition shown in this photograph, taken in May 1980 when it was passing through Warwick towing the restored FMC butty *Northwich*. Original FMC machinery has long since vanished, and *President* is now powered by a 'Scotch' boiler somewhat larger than the original coupled to a two-cylinder simple engine of appropriate age and style. The boat has attended a number of national boat rallies since completion, and in 1980 travelled as far as the River Lea in company with *Northwich*, the latter having just been renovated for the Waterways Museum. Much interest has been created by the steamer, but experience has shown that life on these boats in their heyday was anything but glamorous. Both crews and boats led a hard life, and it is easy to appreciate the reasons for changing to diesel power once a suitable engine appeared on the market (*R. J. Blenkinsop*)

Jonathan Hulls is reputed to have tried a steamboat on the Warwickshire Avon in the 1730s, so it is appropriate to end our story on these same waters with a photograph of the steam launch *Puffin* at Wyre Mill, Pershore, in 1959. *Puffin* was built by the Liquid Fuel Engineering Co Ltd of East Cowes in 1898, and in her original form had a three-drum, paraffin-fired Lifu water-tube boiler, worked at 250psig, and a Lifu two-cylinder piston-valve compound developing some 35hp and capable of propelling her at around 17 knots. As built she had only the fore-cabin, but at a later date was fitted with an after cabin and it was in this form that five members of the Lower Avon Navigation Trust found her out of use at Burslem in 1956. They were looking for a boat suitable for use in connection with restoration work on the Warwickshire Avon and decided that *Puffin* could be restored for that purpose. The original boiler was beyond repair, so a Merryweather Valiant 'C' vertical boiler was fitted, considerably smaller than the original but capable of producing a reasonable performance. This was at first fitted with Merryweather's own oil-firing gear, then converted to coal and finally fitted with a modern oil-firing system based on standard Lucas industrial equipment. Restoration was completed in 1959 and the boat remained on the Avon until 1966, being then moved to the Hamble River where it was advertised for sale during 1981 (*the late Ben Hooper, Collection C. P. Weaver*)

ACKNOWLEDGEMENTS

In compiling a record of steam craft that spans some two centuries, we have of necessity consulted many organisations and individuals in search of documentary or pictorial evidence. To list everybody who has contributed to a project that began more than fifteen years ago is almost impossible and we realise that the list given here is far from complete. To all who have helped us, we offer our sincere thanks; omission from the list does not indicate neglect or forgetfulness: Dr Jean Lindsay, Drs Scott and Hilary Pereira, Messrs Gordon Biddle, Malcolm Braine, Leslie G. Brooks, Kenneth P. Clark, Hugh Compton, Charles Hadfield, John Hemelryke, Brian Hillsdon, Humphrey G. W. Household, C. M. Marsh (former Engineer & Manager, River Weaver Navigation), David McDougall, Derek Mills, Peter Norton, John Norris, Edward Paget-Tomlinson, the late L. T. C. Rolt, Allan Smith, Mike Taylor, A. Urquhart, D. W. Vickerage, John Watson, the late Frank Whyte (former Engineer & Manager, Caledonian Canal) and J. W. Willans. We wish to thank Mr R. J. Blenkinsop for reading through and commenting upon the draft of this book.

We offer special thanks to: Alan H. Faulkner, for assistance with information and illustrations of many waterways, also for his support and encouragement; Graham Langmuir, for making freely available his comprehensive records of Scottish and other steamers; Tony Conder, Roy Jamieson and the late Charles N. Hadlow, of the Waterways Museum, Stoke Bruerne.

Libraries and Record Offices

British Library, Reference Division
British Library, Newspaper Division
National Library of Scotland, Edinburgh
British Transport Historical Records
County of Avon Library HQ, Bristol
City of Birmingham Central Reference Library
Dumfries County Council Libraries
Hillingdon Borough Library
Kenilworth Library
Somerset County Records Office
Strathkelvin District Council, Reference and Local History Section
Suffolk County Council Records Office

Periodicals

The Engineer
Engineering
Gentleman's Magazine
Illustrated London News
Motor Boat & Yachting
The Scots Magazine

Museums and Art Galleries

National Maritime Museum, Greenwich
Welsh Industrial & Maritime Museum, Cardiff
Dundee Museums & Art Galleries
Exeter Maritime Museum
Glasgow Museums & Art Galleries
University of Reading, Museum of English Rural Life

Other Organisations

British Waterways Board staff at Ardrishaig, Gloucester, Inverness, Leeds and Northwich
Patent Office, London
Patent Library, Birmingham
Janes Fighting Ships
Lloyd's Register of Shipping
County of South Glamorgan Fire Service
F. T. Everard & Sons Ltd
Fisons Ltd
Charles Hill, Bristol, Ltd
Imperial Chemical Industries Ltd
Manchester Ship Canal Company